The
Christian Teacher

The
Christian Teacher

By

Clarence H. Benson, LITT. D.

FORMERLY, DIRECTOR OF THE CHRISTIAN EDUCATION
COURSE AT THE MOODY BIBLE INSTITUTE OF CHICAGO.
SECRETARY OF THE EVANGELICAL TEACHER TRAIN-
ING ASSOCIATION. FOUNDER OF THE ALL BIBLE
GRADED SERIES AND THE SUPERIOR
SUMMER SCHOOL SERIES

MOODY PRESS

CHICAGO

Introduction

SINCE 1926 the Sunday school enrollment in Britain and America has not advanced as it did in earlier years. More than six and one-half million pupils have dropped out of their classes in the United States and Canada alone. While the decline has been arrested in recent years, and some of the small denominations are making sensational gains, it will take a long time for the Sunday school to regain its former size and prestige.

One surprising fact, which should be a source of great encouragement, is the unprecedented additions to the teaching staff. Strange as it may seem, while the Sunday school has been losing pupils, it has been gaining teachers. This was first revealed by the government census of 1936, which announced for the previous decade a gain of 93,892 teachers, despite the loss of 2,649,542 pupils. The International Council of Religious Education, in its compilation of statistics between 1944 and 1947, discovered that there was a gain of 613,289 teachers. Whereas three years ago the average class consisted of 14 pupils, there is now one teacher for every 10 pupils.

What is the explanation for this greatly increased teaching staff? Why does the Sunday school today have more teachers than at any time in its history? This question is not difficult to answer. The Evangelical Teacher Training Association has had a steady growth since coming into existence in May, 1931. It now has 161 schools offering its courses. Most of the listed Bible institutes, colleges, and seminaries are interdenominational, so that its ministry has reached into the churches of practically all the major bodies, as well as become the inspiration of many of the small denominations. It has sponsored perennial rather than spasmodic training, and its graduates have received a preparation that compares favorably with that which normal schools provide for public school teachers. These graduates are fully equipped to conduct training classes where institutional training is not available. More teachers eventually mean more pupils, and better teachers of course mean better Sunday schools. If every one of these graduates who now holds a diploma conducted a training class—and many of them are doing this—one can well understand why there are these additional teachers, and how far-reaching are the possibilities of the Sunday school's regaining its lost ground. The Southern Baptist Convention is doing a notable work also.

Since its beginning, the Association has used my texts in *Child Study* and *Sunday School Administration,* and abridgements of these form the manuals of the Preliminary Training Course. To complete the six units of this course, I also prepared a manual in *Pedagogy.* Ever since, there has been a persistent demand that the teachers be provided with an unabridged text which could also be used by the students in the Standard Training Course. *The Christian Teacher* is my response. This text, I trust, will be as useful as *Introduction to Child Study,* which has now run into fifteen printings in addition to an English edition. The chapter on *Observation and Practice Teaching* will be of special interest to those students who were in my classes when I was Director of the Christian Education Course at Moody Bible Institute. These helpful young people not only assisted materially in the production of the *All Bible Graded Series* of Sunday school lessons, and the *Superior Summer School Series* for Vacation Bible School, but were instrumental, in their practice teaching, for providing many helpful suggestions for the manual on *Pedagogy.*

In all of my texts on Christian education, I have earnestly

endeavored to magnify the teaching ministry. This contribution will have adequately fulfilled its purpose if the all-important work of the teacher is recognized and appreciated.

Our Lord must have had the teacher particularly in mind when He spake the parable of the sower. Here He answered an important question—"If the gospel is from God, why is it not more effective?" Well, there is nothing wrong with the Sower, who is the Son of God, or the Seed, which is the Word of God. The difficulty lies in the soil, and in the sowing of the seed, which has been intrusted to the teacher's hands. The seed scattered by the evangelist is so often "too little and too late," but the sowing of the patient, plodding teacher will eventually take root and reappear with the promise of a harvest. It takes time and patience to press beyond the mind and reach the soul and spirit of the individual. Only as the teacher thus approaches his task is there any assurance that the good seed will not only get down into the soil, but also will have a resurrection in a transformed and fruitful life.

C.H.B.

Contents

9

Part I: *The Task*

1

Reaching the Mentality

WHAT is a teacher? A teacher is one who helps somebody else to learn. In other words, the teacher cooperates with the pupil in learning. He does not seek to perform before an audience made up of listening pupils, but undertakes with them an activity in which they are busily engaged. There is no teaching unless there is learning. The teacher has not really taught unless the pupil has learned. The *object* of our teaching is to make something happen in the life of our pupil. The *test* of our teaching is what happens in the life of our pupil.

The pupil-teacher relationship is all-important. Whether or not the teacher is primarily a helper in the learning process, will depend not only upon the teacher's interest in his instruction, but also upon the pupil's attitude towards his teacher. A pupil will not receive much help from a teacher he does not like. Teachers will never interest pupils in anything in which they are not themselves interested. A teacher can render help by guiding a pupil. One who has been over the road can best direct the footsteps of the traveler who is taking it for the first time. The teacher can also help by inspiring the pupil. In his pupils the teacher is so frequently confronted with laziness, indifference and ignorance. This resistance to learning challenges all the patience and resources

13

of the instructor. A teacher is co-operating with his pupil in helping him to learn when he can arouse that pupil to share his own interest in the instruction.

How does the task of the religious teacher compare with that of the secular teacher? The work of instruction in the Sunday school is much more difficult than in the public school. Religion and morals are more difficult to teach than arithmetic and geography. The lesson materials are not so well graded and adapted as the public school texts. The lessons are taught weekly, instead of daily, and the time for instruction is brief. Children do not prepare their lessons, and so come to class lacking the background of knowledge and the mental alertness so essential for receiving instruction.

How does the task of the Christian teacher compare with that of the religious teacher? Christian teaching is much more than religious teaching. Religious teaching finds its materials anywhere and everywhere. Hymns, prayers, poetry, paintings and sculpture, the themes of which are religious, things of beauty in the natural world, vocational problems, social problems, political problems, economic problems, and problems of every imaginable sort are put into the curriculum of religious education, with a view to making lessons life-centered. "Religious education has appropriated much from secular education, without being conscious of the fact that the latter is too young to be a trustworthy source from which to borrow." [1] Secular education deals with the material, while religious teaching is concerned with the spiritual. Religious education magnifies technique at the expense of content. Christian teaching realizes its responsibility for the proclamation of the gospel message, and therefore does not permit the message to be eclipsed by the method.

While Christian teaching recognizes that there are sources of spiritual inspiration and guidance outside of Scripture, it

[1] C. B. Eavey, *Principles of Teaching for Christian Teachers*, p. 14.

gives the Bible the supreme place. For it, the Bible is the infallible, inspired Word of the eternal God, given to man to reveal his destiny and the plan for his salvation. By the Bible the thoughts of men will be judged, the works of men will be rewarded, and the lives of men are to be guided.

The task of the Christian teacher may be divided into three parts or objectives. Failure will follow not only the neglect to reach all of the objectives, but also the attempt to reach them out of their proper order. The three objectives may be compared with the three divisions of the human being—body, soul, and spirit. The majority of psychologists, especially those who reject the Bible, do not concede that man is a threefold creation. They divide him into body and soul, and the latter generally includes the mind. The Bible reveals a threefold nature. Both soul and spirit refer to the immaterial part of man, but from different points of view. The distinction between the threefold divisions may be better understood when we speak of the body as having world-consciousness, the soul, self-consciousness, and the spirit, God-consciousness.

World-consciousness concerns a knowledge of the things about us. Through his five senses man is constantly gathering information and learning many things about this marvelous world in which he lives.

The distinguishing factor between the human race and brute creation is the mind. It is that part of the body so mysteriously distinct—man's intellectual powers—to which the teacher is to make his first approach. In reaching the mentality, the teacher's object is to stimulate the acquisition and assimilation of knowledge.

I. ACQUISITION OF KNOWLEDGE

1. Sensation
Sensation is the great door through which the knowledge of the outer world comes into the mind. For this purpose, we

find, the body and mind are closely connected. Throughout
the body there is a vast network of nerves which connect with
the brain, the center of the nervous system. The five senses
have been called the "royal roads to the mind." Information
is being constantly gathered by means of the eye-gate and
the ear-gate, and the senses of taste and touch and smell. The
teacher can awaken and stimulate the senses. Thus he quick-
ens the acquisition of knowledge. A man may walk through
the world with his eyes open, and yet not see. Sailors may
travel around the world and know very little of it beyond
certain places of amusement. On the other hand, Benjamin
Franklin, with senses ever alert for picking up information,
could not cross the English Channel without making observations that were useful to mankind.

2. Perception

Perception is the ability to interpret the information given
by sensations. In sensations one is aware of the existence of
an object. In perception the object is given a distinct meaning,
that is, the distant object is recognized as an automobile.

"Sensations are the raw material of knowledge. Percepts
are the first objects made from this raw material. If sensations
be likened to iron ore, then percepts may be likened to iron
bars and sheets from it." [2]

Apperception is the perception of things in relation to
ideas we already possess. This is one of the basic principles
of learning. Only through relation and comparison with the
known can we grasp and understand the unknown.

II. ASSIMILATION OF KNOWLEDGE

The acquisition of knowledge for the intellect is similar to
the acquisition of food for the body. When we sit down to
partake of food, our primary object is acquisition. Knowledge,

[2] O. M. Norlie, *An Elementary Christian Psychology*, p. 89.

in the same way, is acquired through the five gates provided for that purpose. In the partaking of food we have only begun the process in accomplishing the real purpose for which we eat. While it may be true of some people that they live to eat, the majority eat to live. The food enters the body. What is now necessary in order that it may be a real contribution to life? God in His wisdom has prepared, in the human body, digestive organs which enable the body to assimilate the food acquired.

There is a definite purpose for partaking of food, so also we have a real object in obtaining knowledge. Knowledge is power, but in order that it may be harnessed and put to work, it is necessary to do more than acquire it. Knowledge to be retained must be assimilated. For this purpose we possess memory. Memory records, retains, recalls, and recognizes past experiences.

1. Recording of knowledge

This recording process is sometimes called memorizing, or learning by heart. We can write most successfully on the mind of a child because the storehouse of knowledge is not yet crowded with a multitude of facts. A sense of duty is a fine incentive to recording facts, as practice is in trusting one's memory. Memory grows in trustworthiness, by being trusted. Strong, as well as repeated impressions live through memory. Vividness of impressions, especially with children, is due to primacy. The first visit to the city, the first day of school, make a deep impression. Special occasions such as Christmas, and birthday anniversaries, will register strongly in the mind. Were these occasions more frequent, their record would be less vivid.

2. Retention of knowledge

Even more important than power to record, is power to retain. In the study of psychology and pedagogy there has been no faculty of the mind so emphasized as memory, and no phase of memory more stressed than retention. Marvelous feats of memory have been recorded. Cyrus the Great could name every soldier in his army! An outstanding actor could repeat word for word the columns of a newspaper, after reading them. Petrus D. Ravenna recited all the sermons that had been given in his hearing during lent.[3] A well-known mathematician was able to write long columns of figures upon a blackboard as they were given to him by the audience and then turn around and repeat them backwards from last to first. Harry Nelson Pillsbury, the great American chess player, was able to play, blindfolded, with a dozen men, and win every game. On one occasion, in pointing out a mistake, he was able to recall every move that had been made without seeing the chessboard.

3. Recalling of knowledge

Frequent repetitions made according to plan and purpose, are an excellent aid to successful recall. But the call should be made on the same track over which it has originally come. Knowledge, to be recalled, must be taken gradually. The brain like the stomach must have rest between meals. Students who hastily force study for final examinations never do as well as those who master the daily assignment. Instruction that can be introduced by a survey of the whole, can much more readily be recalled, because it provides in advance a connected view of the entire subject.

4. Recognition of knowledge

Recognition is the identification of knowledge and the ability to relate it to previous information. Thus a tune heard before is recognized and identified.

Memory is absolutely necessary for apperception [clear perception]. We cannot compare or relate new impressions with

[3] Norlie, *op. cit.,* p. 79.

old unless we can recall them. With memory, our mind can project itself backward and forward through time and space, and the events of today can be understood and enjoyed by the experiences of yesterday. Memory, therefore, has well been called a tax-gatherer of the past, and a treasurer of the mind.[4] The older we become, the more we are prone to indulge in reminiscences. Augustine, in his *Confessions,* cried, "Great is this power of memory, exceeding great, O my God—an inner chamber large and boundless."

QUESTIONS

1. What is a teacher?
2. What is meant by the pupil-teacher relationship?
3. How does the task of the religious teacher compare with that of the secular teacher?
4. How does the task of the Christian teacher compare with that of the religious teacher?
5. What are the three objectives of the Christian teacher?
6. What may be said of the distinction between the body, soul, and mind?
7. What are the two objects of the teacher in reaching the mentality?
8. What does the teacher have to do with sensation?
9. Distinguish between sensation and perception.
10. In what four ways does memory assimilate knowledge?
11. Mention several outstanding feats of memory.
12. Why is memory necessary for apperception?

[4] Norlie, *op. cit.,* p. 100.

2

Reaching the Personality

WE HAVE seen that the teacher is one who helps somebody else to learn. We have also seen that the learner has a capacity for knowledge, and have noted the means by which it is acquired and assimilated. We have been studying man's marvelous intellectual equipment, and the means by which knowledge can be introduced and preserved. But, while we have been reaching man's mechanism, we have not reached man. It is one thing to teach the Bible, and quite another to teach John. The fundamental of teaching is getting a response. It is quite possible to store the mind with knowledge and even stimulate the memory to retain it without in any way affecting the individual.

I. DEFINING PERSONALITY

1. The immaterial being

What is personality? In the first chapter we said that the human being was a triad creature, composed of body, soul, and spirit, and that while the body was the instrument for *world*-consciousness, the soul was the expression of *self*-consciousness. The soul is the immaterial, invisible, immortal part of man. It was created by God and placed in the body of clay that He had made. It was not made of dust, and does not return to dust.

"Dust thou art, to dust returnest,
Was not spoken of the soul."

In the process of creation, man became a "living soul" (Gen. 2:7). I am a "living soul," but I have a body which is "dust of the ground." The body is the machine, but the soul is the machinist. The body is man's servant. Through it he learns the facts about the physical universe, and with it he adjusts himself to the world in which he lives, or makes the world over to conform with his ideals. Man is not the slave of his environment.

We need not be disturbed because we cannot describe the soul or locate it in our physical organism. Sometimes it seems to be wholly resident in the body, for it drives the body and in turn is affected by the body. Again, as in dreams and imaginations, it seems to be able to transcend the body.

Old Testament writers do not try to define the soul, although they assume its existence. They speak of the longing soul, the thirsty soul, the sorrowing soul, the striving soul. Their use of the word makes it synonymous with man's real self. It is affirmed but never argued that the soul derives its existence from God, therefore it is imperishable. Man is more than a cunningly devised organism of muscle, nerves and brain cells. He is a God-given individual, with the power of choice, will, and self-control.

Personality exists where there is intelligence, feeling or emotion, and will. It is more than mere consciousness that is possessed by an animal. It is *self*-consciousness. It is more than mere determination, since even animals determine their actions in the light of external circumstances. Man has *self*-determination, or the power to act in accordance with his own free will, which is frequently contrary to the influence of external circumstances.

2. The sovereign being

Bodies differ from each other, and it is impossible for us to find two that are exactly alike in every detail of construction. Even twins will have some physical difference which enables us to distinguish them. But even if it were possible to find two bodies exactly alike, we have yet to discover the duplicate of the soul. In fact, we generally distinguish twins by personality traits rather than physical differences.

One of the most profound thoughts for mankind is that each individual has been created directly and differently. His personality is distinctive, and when he does not attempt to ape someone else he comes to be recognized and appreciated because he can be distinguished from everyone else. We find not only that the soul is not duplicated, but that each is highly privileged. The mechanic can have absolute control over the machine, no matter how complicated it may be. This, likewise, is the soul's privilege and power.

Above all, man has a will that is entirely his own. Will is the name for the mind's power to act. It is personal, and ties persons and things to itself. In an active will man conceives of himself as having dominion over other selves or other objects. The will is the personal self, conscious of its power over its environment. It moves everything else to suit its own purpose. It transforms people and things to its own ends. A dominant will exercises great power over other wills.

II. CONTACTING PERSONALITY

How does the teacher contact the personality? He must do more than hear a recitation. A lesson is not necessarily learned when it has been committed to memory. Even when the pupil understands the meaning of the words memorized by him, it may be only a rote-recitation that he gives to his teacher. The lesson may have reached his mind, but not his soul.

Dr. H. Clay Trumbull tells of an experience he had when a young man teaching a Sunday school class of wide-awake boys.[1] It was in the days of the old question book, long before the advent of the uniform lesson. The book used was one in which every answer was printed out in full just below the question. The ordinary practice of the pupil was to memorize the answers, while the teacher's task was to hear the recitation.

Now it happened on a certain Sunday, the lesson was "The Walk to Emmaus," and the first question was, Where is Emmaus? As Dr. Trumbull started to ask the first question, he recalled that the pupil on his right had been absent the previous Sunday. So instead of asking the anticipated question in the book, he inquired, "Where were you last Sunday, John?" Quick as a flash the answer came back, "Seven and a half miles northwest of Jerusalem." "Well," said his teacher, "you certainly are excused for not being here." But, Dr. Trumbull points out, the lesson he learned that day was that hearing a recitation could by no means be called teaching. The memorizing of words is in itself no more the securing of ideas than is the buying of books the securing of knowledge. Teaching is not complete unless it in some way affects or influences the pupil.

1. The receptive contact

Teachers whose only aim is to reach the mentality are making only a receptive contact with their pupils. This is a common teaching practice, whereby one seeks to hand down to the learner an accumulated stock of knowledge and learning.

When I was teaching in the higher commercial school of Kobe, Japan, I noticed that my Japanese students were accustomed to take copious notes, writing down verbatim al-

[1] Trumbull, *Teaching and Teachers*, p. 19.

most every word they heard in the classroom. These were later copied into a vast array of notebooks. By the time the student graduated, he would have accumulated several shelves of well-filled volumes. On one occasion a graduate carefully packed away these valuable notebooks in a large trunk, which was later taken down to the wharf to be placed in the boat in which he was to embark for his home in Tokyo. In getting the trunk on board with some other baggage, the rope broke and the trunk plunged into the sea. The heart-broken, bewildered student gazed upon the sad catastrophe and then telegraphed his father, "I do not know what to do; I have lost my education." He had acquired knowledge without appropriating it.

2. The responsive contact

In sharp contrast to the receptive contact is the responsive contact. It deals with persons. Its end is the growth and culture of persons, the enrichment of their character, and the enlargement of their outlook on life. A responsive contact is made when you give first consideration to the interests and understanding of your pupils, and the questions which they ask. Your aim will be not only to secure a response from the pupil, but to make him feel responsible for his instruction.

A study of the nervous system will better enable us to understand our objective. Running from the brain in all directions is a double set of wires, which transmit the most delicate stimuli. One of these wires is the sensory nerve. Its function is to carry communications to the brain. Paralleling it is the motor nerve, which conveys the return communication from the brain. The sensory nerve receives the impression, the motor nerve returns the expression. The sensory nerve is the servant of external influence. The motor nerve is the executive of the personality.

It can readily be seen that while part of the mechanism of

the human body is for the purpose of receiving impressions, an equal amount has been reserved for the use of the operator. Getting a response or reply to our impression is an evidence of life. In the dark I stumble over the dog. Almost immediately there is an expression to my impression. But that yelp of the dog, while an evidence of life, is not an intelligent or individualistic expression. Only impressions that stimulate an intelligent response are the evidences of a personality. Leadership will be developed in proportion to the opportunity we give in our program for individual thought and expression.

3. Teaching that interests

The teacher has reached the mentality when he has imparted information, but his contact with the personality will depend upon interest.

Attention is the first response of a personality to the stream of knowledge that is flowing through his senses. In another chapter more will be said about the importance of gaining attention. However, it is difficult if not impossible to *sustain* attention without interest.

Interest sometimes has to be created, but generally it is alert and curious about anything that concerns self. It is strictly a personal relationship.

a. Personal information

Dr. A. H. McKinney illustrates this with the account of a lady walking on the beach of one of our popular summer resorts.[2] Her attention was attracted by a group of persons some distance away. The group soon increased to a crowd. On inquiring, she learned that the body of a man had just been recovered from the waves. Pressing forward to learn more, she was startled to find that it was her own son. Mere attention was instantly changed to deep interest, for she had been touched at a vital spot.

[2] McKinney, *Practical Pedagogy in the Sunday School,* p. 97.

Newspapers understand the value of the personal field. The slogan of many a country paper is, "Every name in print a subscriber." The country editor has learned that his subscribers are primarily interested in having their names appear in his paper even if they are not connected with any extraordinary happenings. What has to do with ourselves and our immediate friends will always command our interest. Teaching that interests must be related to the everyday life of the pupils. The teacher who does not know the everyday life of his pupils has no point of contact through which to interest them.

b. Comprehensive information

Interest will never attach to what the mind cannot grasp. It is like the static that comes over the radio and prevents a clear hearing of the broadcast. Language chosen to express the thought may not have been sufficiently simple to be understood. Empty words devoid of meaning will never stimulate interest. Information that is beyond the grasp of intelligence cannot secure interest even if provided in language that can be understood. It may concern matters with which there has been no previous contact. Information must have sufficient connection with personal experience, and be sufficiently close to things that are known and appreciated if it is to be comprehended. The new must be related to something old and familiar in the mind to meet a warm welcome.

c. Living information

The soul is the expression of life. It is only natural then that interest attaches to action. It is the movement we detect in the window display that arrests our attention more than the beautiful decorations and the unique design. Words of action captivate more quickly than adjectives of explanation and description. The story that is full of life and movement makes stronger appeal than a beautiful painting. The soul not only responds to life, but seeks to put life into others. The reason we learn by doing is that we are more interested in doing than we are in listening. All good teaching, therefore, will appeal to interest by providing the fullest possible opportunity for participation in the lesson. The pupil is not only interested in living things, but is anxious to make his own contribution to keep them alive.

d. *Vivacious presentation*

Life begets life. A teacher who is full of life is seldom troubled by lack of interest and attention. The teacher is the model unconsciously accepted and imitated by his class. He leads the way in interest. A mechanical and lifeless teacher cannot command interest. After all, a great school must be the expression of great personalities. It is the pupil's contact with life and not with books or inanimate things that really affects his own life. It is hard for us to realize how successfully the apostles and their successors carried on by an oral ministry. Textbooks were unknown and even the words of the Lord Jesus were not committed to writing until thirty years after His resurrection. But the apostolic school was the burning expression of great personalities. Their characters were caught, not taught, and the world's contact with their lives and not their books made an indelible impression upon it.

III. DEVELOPING THE PERSONALITY

1. Appropriation of knowledge

Let us again refer to the physical realm. We eat to live, but the acquisition and even the assimilation of food has not as yet contributed to that end. It must be appropriated to be of any real value. God has marvelously arranged the mechanism of the body so that when food is properly digested, it is taken up by the blood and carried to the extremities, to restore worn out portions. Thus the food eaten and digested actually becomes a part of us.

In the same way, only when knowledge is appropriated and enters into our life sufficiently to govern and influence our acts is it of any personal value. The teacher has not finished his task when he has taught his class so much subject matter —so many facts, maxims or lessons. Indeed he shall need to teach them all these things and teach them well, but he must ask himself, What have these things done for the boys and girls of my class? What has been the outcome of my teaching? How much effect has it had on their life, character, and conduct? The evidence of real learning is to be found in the changes or modifications of behavior that occur in the life of the learner. In other words, has the teaching-learning process made a difference in the pupil?

How do we know knowledge has been appropriated? Largely from the response that is secured from the question "Why?" As long as one is content to use the word "What" in making his inquiries, replies may be only factual knowledge that has been acquired and stored in the library of the human intellect. But when the question "Why?" is asked, the operator must do more than tap his resources of knowledge. He must express himself.

a. Expressing an opinion

Knowledge is appropriated when a personal opinion has been expressed. "I think" is the response of the individual to his reaction to the inquiry. The solicitation of personal opinion will call for self-expression, and constitute a distinct contribution of the personality.

When our Lord was seeking self-expression on the part of His disciples upon the all-important matter of His deity, His first question was of an impersonal nature, "Whom do men

say that I am?" There were various replies. One had heard
that He was Elijah, another, Jeremiah, while undoubtedly
several reported that He was known as a prophet. So far our
Lord was simply gathering information from His disciples.
But now He makes a personal and direct appeal, "Whom say
ye that I am?" The answer of the spokesman Peter was the
recognition of the Twelve that He was the Christ, the Son of
the living God.

b. Expressing a desire

Our feelings, as well as our opinions when expressed, betray our personality. Our desires may include wishes, longings,
and hankerings. The wish is a less vehement form of desire.
A longing is an impatient and continued species of desire. A
hankering is a desire for that which is out of one's reach.

Deliberation occurs when there are conflicting desires. It
is a process in which each conflicting desire pleads its own
cause before the soul. One argues, "Take a drink—the taste is
good." The other argues, "Do not take a drink—the conse-
quences will be bad." Deliberation takes times. It is a state of
hesitation. Deliberation implies uncertainty. It is a state of
doubt.[3]

Choice is the power to decide between clamorous desires.
The "Shall I?" or "Shall I not?" of deliberation, is settled for
the time being and perhaps for all time. When two courses
are opened, choice is the power of the personality to decide to
take one rather than the other. Within limitations, self is free
to choose. However, unless choice is a free act, the will is not
a free agent. The Declaration of Independence proclaimed
that all men were created equal and therefore were entitled
to freedom of choice.

Purpose is prolonged choice. Just as choice is preceded by
deliberation, it is followed by a struggle to maintain itself un-

[3] Norlie, *An Elementary Christian Psychology,* p. 133.

til action takes place.[4] In this democracy where freedom of opportunity abounds, the chief executives in many instances chose to be president long before they were elected to their high office. But their choice was followed by a resolution which developed into a purpose in which they persevered until they attained their goal.

2. Application of knowledge

We had a purpose in partaking of food at the dinner table. The food, as we have seen, was necessary to repair worn-out tissues of the body. Therefore, it was our activity that required the provision of the bodily needs and the renewing of our strength. Man needs food to sustain him in his activities, and the active man generally possesses a good appetite for his meals.

It is the application or use of knowledge which is the real end of education. It is not the knowledge we acquire, but what we utilize that affects the personality.

a. Personality strengthened by experience

We learn by doing. It is possible to have a good choice and a noble purpose without carrying them out in action. Action is the capability to do what we determine to do.[5] Action is the execution of the choice. Experience is the best teacher, but we also grow by doing. We develop through experiences. Every time use is made of knowledge acquired, the personality is strengthened. We are all reacting agents to impressions, developing our own personality by our own activity. Since expression is the action of the executive, constant expression develops his personal powers. When some particular act which he has appropriated is indulged in again and again, it becomes a habit. Habitual actions are tendencies to repeat what has been done before, time and again. "As the twig is bent, so the

---

[4] Norlie, *op. cit.*, p. 134.
[5] Norlie, *op. cit.*, p. 134.

tree is inclined." A lazy youth, a slothful man. Every act performed leaves its trace along the pathway, and every repetition deepens the trace.

b. Personality established by habit

Descartes claimed that individual thought is the evidence of the personality, but the power to think and act individually is necessarily dependent upon the acquisitions of habits of thought and action. We can form habits of thinking and acting that will forcibly influence our own thoughts and actions. Most actions are in some degree controlled by individual thought. The mechanical contribution of habit is always personal.

There is no greater reflector of the individual than his habits. Habit is that which enables us to do easily, readily and with growing certainty that which we do often. Every act leaves in the structure of the body and mind a capacity to repeat itself. This tendency to repeat movements and thoughts is habit. Bad habits are our most persistent enemies. Good habits are our most helpful friends. The most important thing in all education is to make our habits our ally instead of our enemy.

IV. PERFECTING PERSONALITY

History records the achievements of its great men. It is well to observe however, that while volumes may be written about good men and bad men, little is said about weak men. Only the reigns of kings who possessed the requisites for leadership and ruled with a strong hand occupy a conspicuous place in the pages of history. A dominating personality requires a strong will—one that overcomes obstacles, conquers temptations, and wins victories over natural propensities. A weak will is a negative will that forgets its ideals, yields to temptation, is deaf to duty and follows the line of least resistance.

The sluggard, the drunkard, and the coward are all types of the weak-willed. Perfect control and accurate execution are evidences of strong will.[6]

QUESTIONS

1. What is personality?
2. How did the Old Testament use of the word "soul" imply personality?
3. In what respects is man a sovereign being?
4. Distinguish between the receptive contact and the responsive contact.
5. In what respects does the nervous system become the executive of the personality?
6. What is the key to gaining and sustaining attention?
7. In what four ways can interest be stimulated?
8. What is meant by vivacious presentation?
9. In what two ways can a personality be developed?
10. How do we know when knowledge has been appropriated?
11. What do deliberation, choice, and purpose have to do in the expressing of a desire?
12. How can personality be strengthened and established?

[6] Norlie, *op. cit.*, p. 136.

3

Reaching the Spirituality

THUS FAR we have considered the task of every teacher, first to reach the mentality and then the personality. But the Christian teacher must go further than this. He must reach the spiritual nature—the God-consciousness of man.

Of the three planes of life, the highest is the plane of God; the central, the plane of man; the lowest, the plane of the beast. Two great facts are revealed by a study of these planes:

1. The animal *cannot* ascend to the plane of man. This is one of the strongest arguments against evolution. Here is an impassable chasm.

2. Man can pass from one plane to another. His endowment of self-determination enables him to sit like a king between heaven and earth. He can descend and live on the plane of the beast, or he can rise to heavenly places and hold communion with God.

Christianity teaches us that there is only one Supreme Being —God. God has manifested Himself through the book of Nature as well as through the book of sacred Scripture.

"The heavens declare the glory of God; and the firmament sheweth his handywork. Day unto day uttereth speech, and night unto night sheweth knowledge. There is no speech nor language, where their voice is not heard . . . The law of the Lord is perfect, converting the soul: the testimony of the Lord is sure, making wise the simple" (Ps. 19:1-3, 7).

Above all, God has revealed Himself to man through His only begotten Son.

"God, who at sundry times and in divers manners spake in time past unto the fathers by the prophets, hath in these last days spoken unto us by his Son, whom he hath appointed heir of all things, by whom also he made the worlds; who being the brightness of his glory, and the express image of his person . . ." (Heb. 1:1-3).

Now, while men may learn about God through their senses, in the same way as they have been conscious of the world about them, these faculties are not sufficient for a personal or soul acquaintance with Him. There are other means which must be employed if God is to become a reality in every thought and life. One of these is

I. FAITH

1. Definition

The Bible defines it as "the substance of things hoped for, the evidence of things not seen" (Heb. 11:1). Faith is sometimes called a sixth sense, to be employed especially in the spiritual realm. It is not to be exercised independent of the five senses through which man acquires knowledge. It is rather as a supplementary avenue through which he can penetrate realms inaccessible to the five senses. Faith in its widest sense is belief in what another states, simply on the ground of his truthfulness. It is dependence upon a person or thing as trustworthy. Faith is within the reach of the lowest intelligence, and makes its appeal to the keenest intellect. The vine clinging to the tree is a type of it. The infant in its mother's arms is an example of it. Faith, in a narrower sense, is the religious faculty of the soul. It is the power to believe in God and to fear, love, trust, adore, reverence, and worship Him. There are two kinds of religious faith:

a. Natural faith

Natural religious faith is the power to worship a Higher Being.[1] Every human being, even in his natural corrupt state has this religious faculty. The natural man is corrupt on account of having inherited a sinful nature. When Adam sinned, he lost the image of God and passed sin and death on to his posterity. His whole being was poisoned with sin, and his understanding became dark. Despite his sinful and lost estate, man has ever retained a certain belief that there is a God. He has possessed a certain longing, although secret perhaps, for the worship that was forfeited by Adam's transgression. This natural religious faculty, like the other powers of the soul, is of high value, although it is corrupt and cannot save a man.

Evolutionists say that all religious ideas, including that of God, have been the result of a process of natural improvement. This is contrary to God's Word. Man was created with a religious faculty. Our first parents knew the Creator to be a true God. After sin came into the world, this knowledge became more and more dim. Men began to worship the things God had created instead of the Creator. Instead of man evolving from a crude beginning to a higher level, the Bible shows that wherever he has been left to himself, his religion, as well as his morals, has degenerated.

b. Supernatural faith

God, in the eternal counsel, has made provision for man's salvation—in the fullness of time the Lord Jesus Christ came to save. He saves from sin and death and eternal punishment those who believe on Him as their Saviour.

This faith in Christ is supernatural faith, or Christian

[1] Norlie, *An Elementary Christian Psychology,* p. 162.

faith.[2] It is the firm conviction of the truth of what God has revealed in the Bible. It believes that God and His Word are trustworthy. It relies wholly upon God and His promises of salvation through Christ. While natural religious faith is common to all men, supernatural faith is possessed only by those in whom the regeneration of the Holy Spirit has created an unshakable belief in the Lord Jesus Christ.

In natural religious faith there is a feeling of hostility to God, "because the carnal mind is enmity against God" (Rom. 8:7). The natural mind is afraid of God, with the fear of a slave or of a criminal. In supernatural faith there is a feeling of love to God "because he first loved us" (I John 4:19). The Christian fears God only in the sense that he fears to displease Him. He cries out with Joseph, "How can I do this great wickedness, and sin against God?" (Gen. 39:9). Christian faith not only transforms fear into love, but also opinion into conviction. Whereas the natural man expresses an opinion, the spiritual man speaks with conviction. Interest that expresses a personality becomes enthusiasm. The word "enthusiasm" literally means "God in you," and strictly speaking is the possession only of those who have supernatural faith.

II. CONSCIENCE

The word "conscience" is seldom heard in a class of modern psychologists.[3] Many psychologists do not believe in the conscience. If they do give it any consideration, they insist that it has been acquired and is not a gift of God. However, the teaching of the Bible is very plain. It states that the Gentiles, who were not the recipients of the law given to the Jews, have "their conscience also bearing witness, and their thoughts the mean while accusing or else excusing one another" (Rom. 2:15).

[2] Norlie, *op. cit.,* p. 164.
[3] Norlie, *op. cit.,* p. 145.

1. Definition

From this passage we must infer that conscience is the voice of God in the human soul. Conscience tells a person what he ought to do and what he ought not to do. It approves of what is right and disapproves of what is wrong in thought and word and deed.

Conscience is the moral faculty of the soul, the power to know and feel and will in matters of right and wrong. The word conscience does not occur in the Old Testament, but appears thirty-two times in the New Testament.[4] Although not mentioned by name, we find evidence of its presence in the Old Testament.

2. Evidences

When Adam and Eve had sinned, they were immediately seized with shame and fear. They went and hid themselves. When Joseph's brethren were called to account by the governor of Egypt, their consciences reminded them of their base treatment of their younger brother. "They said one to another, We are verily guilty concerning our brother, in that we saw the anguish of his soul, when he besought us, and we would not hear; therefore is this distress come upon us" (Gen. 42:21). When Pharaoh of Egypt had his dream, the conscience of the chief butler reminded him of his promise to the imprisoned Joseph. He confessed, "I do remember my faults this day." Conscience was known to the ancient Greeks and Romans. The Greeks pictured an accusing conscience very vividly. The guilty souls were entrusted to three Furies whose hair was made of living snakes, and who drove the culprits with stinging lashes to the underworld abode of the wicked, a place called Tartarus.

It is not necessary to prove that conscience exists and that it is a part of man's birthright. The life, language and literature of every people abound in examples of conscience at

[4] Norlie, *op. cit.*, p. 150.

work. Scarcely anything in the story of mankind has been more conspicuous than the phenomenon of moral distinctions in the world. The massive volumes of history testify to the presence of conscience in every kindred and nation. Every religious system recognizes it. Missionaries declare that even the most benighted heathen are not without moral codes and moral sins. No man need look far to find conscience at work. He can find it in himself. Conscience is a God-given faculty to assist, like faith, in acquainting men with God's righteousness.

3. Judging

Conscience appears as a judge, making accusation against us. This judge is no respecter of persons and makes no distinction between the rich and poor, the ignorant and the intelligent. He persists in accusing us until he has either been obeyed or driven away. Even when silenced for the time being, he is sure to return for another accusation. Thus conscience judges if a man has done evil. But if a man has done what is right, then conscience is quick and sure to approve.

Conscience has been called the "supreme court of the soul." All questions of right and duty are submitted to this court. Here God's laws of righteousness are contrasted with the selfish interests and low standards of men. Here the lawyers argue back and forth with consummate skill and untiring energy until a judgment is rendered. In this trial the conscience is the court room, the prison, the lawyers, the judge, the jury, and the judgment, all in one.[5]

4. Training

a. The Bible

Although conscience is a voice of righteousness within us, it is nevertheless not infallible. It may make mistakes of judgment, and it may reverse its judgment. The conscience clock,

[5] Norlie, *op. cit.*, p. 150.

to keep perfect time, needs to be regulated and corrected. It is commonly accepted that instinct and intelligence are a part of the human being, and they form the basis of his later training and his activities throughout life. But instincts can be perverted. Intelligence can be abused or neglected. In like manner the sense of righteousness can be perverted or neglected.

The world always exercises a strong influence over a weak conscience. The world's standards are imperfect. If conscience is governed by public opinion, sooner or later it will differ from the teaching of God's Word. Just as faith is inspired and quickened by the reading of the Word of God, so conscience is quickened and corrected by God's standards of righteousness. Job's conscience was satisfied in his argument with the three philosophers that he had done no wrong, but when brought face to face with the presence and purity of God, he cried, "I abhor myself, and repent in dust and ashes" (Job 42:6). It required a vision of the Lord sitting upon the throne, high and lifted up, to cause Isaiah to cry, "Woe is me! for I am undone; because I am a man of unclean lips and I dwell in the midst of a people of unclean lips; for mine eyes have seen the King, the Lord of hosts" (Isa. 6:5). It was when Peter had seen the divine power in the miracle of the fishes, that he fell at Jesus' feet, saying, "Depart from me; for I am a sinful man" (Luke 5:8).

b. Environment

While conscience is a God-given gift, it needs to be encouraged in order to be active. Like the still small voice of the Holy Spirit, it can be grieved through inattention and neglect. The alarm clock is a faithful reminder to the early riser, if its voice is always heeded, but one may become unconscious of its presence simply by habitually neglecting to respond to its call.

Conscience then, can be greatly strengthened by environment. At birth, the child possesses no standards of good and
evil. His standards are formed from his environment. If the
environment has been good, his first efforts to depart from it
will be accompanied by pangs of conscience. He has an active
tendency toward the conduct he has learned as good, so that
he cannot take a step far from it without a struggle. Moreover,
his conduct is determined not so much by what he has been
taught, as by what he has observed. It is what the home and
school spontaneously condemn or approve that helps to
strengthen conscience. Public opinion as expressed by parents
and teachers becomes his standard of values, the measure of
his conduct and the reach of his conscience. The conscientious
child is the product of an atmosphere wherein "whatsoever
things are lovely and of good report" are conveyed spontaneously.

III. PRAYER

1. Definition

The Westminster Catechism defines prayer as "an offering
up of our desires unto God, for things agreeable to His will,
in the name of Christ, with confession of our sins and thank-
ful acknowledgment of His mercies." Prayer is spiritual expression. Prayer is the practice of faith in God. Prayer is the
foundation of spiritual life. Prayer is the eternal breath within
the nostrils of men. Dying men seldom pray and the dead
never pray. No one can hold his breath and live. Neither can
one refrain from speaking to God and be alive spiritually.
No man can live whose spinal cord is broken, and no man can
exist spiritually who has severed his connection with heaven.

Prayer is perfectly natural, as breath is to the man who
lives. Man has no great difficulty in breathing except when
dying. He breathes to keep from dying, for he knows that

without breath he will be dead. Living souls cannot easily give up prayer. They will cling to it although they may be obliged to give up everything else. To them it is a matter of life and death. When we pray naturally and easily and continually, we are spiritually alive and well. When we pray infrequently and with difficulty, we are dying. When we cease altogether, we are dead.

2. Importance

Why has God ordained prayer to be the practice of faith in God?

a. Prayer proves the rule of God

God is a King. It is the right of a king to hear and answer the petitions of his subjects. Prayerlessness ignores, if it does not despise, the Ruler of the universe, by refusing to consult or petition Him about any need or grievance. The prayerless man has placed himself outside the pale of civilization by denying to the Ruler the right to hear the petitions of His subjects. If he admits there is a God, while at the same time denying He hears prayer, he has brought his God down to the position of a petty savage chieftain who lives for his own pleasure without regard for the welfare of his subjects.

b. Prayer proves the right of God

God is a Judge. It is the right of a judge to hear and answer the prayer of a plaintiff. For men not to pray to God as the arbitrator of their affairs and the just judge of their adversaries, is an index to the spirit of anarchy. In that state there is no recognition of judicial power, but every man is his own judge and jury. Prayerlessness is ethical anarchy. It ignores or despises the Judge of all the earth by refusing to consult or petition Him about affairs and grievances.

c. Prayer proves the recognition of God

God is a Father. It is right for a father to hear and answer the cry of his child. If you confess the fatherhood of God through the blood atonement of the Lord Jesus Christ, and then deny that He is influenced by the cry of His child, you degrade Him below the level of the beasts and the birds. They heed the cry of their young in distress and hasten to their relief. God must hear the prayer of His child or be branded as infamously heartless. A prayerless man is a Fatherless child. When you pray you prove that you are reconciled to God through the death of Jesus Christ, and God must recognize you as His adopted child by hearing and answering your prayer.

3. Training

While prayer is spiritual expression, and it is possible for a little child to say "Speak, for thy servant heareth," and a wayward sinner to cry, "God be merciful to me a sinner," nevertheless there is much to be learned about this very important subject.

a. Instruction

(1). The Bible

The Bible is perhaps the only book, containing biographical sketches, that has included the prayers of so many of its eminent characters. It does not merely prove the power and give the marvelous results of prayer; it has also included the exact prayers which were used so that they may serve as a pattern to others. Most of these prayers are brief, but the oblation of Solomon at the dedication of the Temple occupies one of the longest chapters in the Bible (I Kings 8) and is a model of style for public worship. Many of the Psalms are models of acceptable devotion. Other parts of Scripture represent God as speaking to man; here man is represented as speaking to God. By these recorded prayers, therefore, we test the utterances and feelings of our hearts, also whether our petitions are expressed in a manner acceptable to God.

Prayers that contain the language of such divine poetry are devotional utterances pleasing to God.

(2). *Christ*

In answer to the question, What rule hath God given for our direction in prayer, reference is again made to the Westminster Catechism which says: "The whole Word of God is of use to direct us in prayer; but the special rule of direction is that form of prayer Christ taught His disciples, commonly called the Lord's Prayer." While commonly called the Lord's Prayer, it would be better to designate it as the "disciples' prayer." That would distinguish it from our Lord's great intercessory prayer in John seventeen. Truly Christ taught His disciples a model prayer, but He also exemplified His instruction by a marvelous life of prayer. The Gospel of Luke records nine distinct occasions when He was *in* prayer. He was praying when He was baptized; when He chose His disciples; at the time of His greatest popularity; at the time of His greatest unpopularity; at the time of His glorification; at the time of His greatest agony; at the time of His greatest physical suffering; at the time of His death, and at the time of His ascension.

b. *Practice*

If prayer is the practice of faith in God, it is necessary that it should early become a part of life.

(1). *Private*

As a child comes to love his parents he may likewise come to love God. His worship will be the expression of his feelings toward the God with whom he has become acquainted through observing the worship of his parents. Gratitude will probably be the underlying cause of his love and reverence. Its expression will be found first in the songs and prayers that he is taught. As soon as a child becomes familiar with the set prayers he has been taught, he may be encouraged to add expressions of personal gratitude, or make petition for some childish need his enlarged experiences may suggest. Sometimes, after asking God's blessing upon father and mother, the child will think of some relative or playmate. Again there will be petitions for something that is on the heart of the little one. These tendencies to individualize his prayer should not be suppressed. They are a manifestation of his unquestioned faith in the power and goodness of God. God in heaven is often very near to the life of a little child.

(2). *Public*

Ability to pray in public is only the natural result of much prayer in private. While the individuality that finds expression when others are not present should not be entirely submerged in formal prayer, nevertheless one must remember that he is *leading* in prayer. It has been well said that in public prayer one either leads or leaves his audience.

Prayer is the most important factor in worship, and training in worship means that Sunday school pupils must really have an opportunity to worship. A part of the Sunday school program must be set apart for this purpose. One learns to worship through worshiping. One learns to pray by praying, and this does not mean listening to someone else pray. The constant consciousness of God in the life must be cultivated. The teacher who comes to have a sense of responsibility for the cultivation of the devotional life of his pupils will wish, in addition to co-operating in the worship service of the Sunday school, to help them in the establishment of the habit of daily private prayer and devotional Bible reading. It is important to create an appreciation of the value of the practice. A given time set apart for private devotion, and held sacred for that purpose, contributes greatly to spiritual life. But when it does so contribute, we may be sure that the observance of that daily hour is something more than mere habit. We must seek to form the habit of daily devotion, not as an end in itself, but as an aid to the cultivation of the spiritual life.

CONCLUSION

We have noted three steps or objectives in the task of the Christian teacher, and that these three objectives may be related to the three divisions of the human being—body, soul, and spirit. We have also noted that it is important for the Christian teacher to take all three steps in reaching the pupil, and to take them in their order.

When the teacher has observed this important law in approaching his task, he will be encouraged to find that what has been merely *instruction* in reaching the mentality, has become *opinion* when he has gone further and contacted the personality, and that through the spiritual aids of faith, conscience, and prayer, opinions have become convictions. The pupil was *intelligent* when his mind was stored with knowledge, but became *interested* when the personality was contacted, and *enthusiastic* when led into the realms of God-consciousness. The pupil may merely *have* (acquisition) if the teacher has only stored his mind with knowledge, but when his interest has been kindled he expresses a *like* or a *dislike*. And when the pupil's spiritual faculties have been reached, his convictions and enthusiasms lead him to *love* or to *hate*.

Knowledge is power, but the acquisition of knowledge in itself does not guarantee success. Knowledge is power only when it is conquered, harnessed, and set to work. Moreover, education is not merely the conquest of knowledge; its reality and finality is the conquest of ourselves. Until a young person's training has brought about the all-important conquest of body and mind, his education is a failure. Knowledge then will not serve us until it has been *conquered*—until we have conquered ourselves. But while the appeal to the personality is the emphasis upon *self-control*, the appeal to the spirituality stresses *God-control*. For it is only God-controlled personalities that can be trusted to exercise self-control.

The teacher who reaches the mentality is preparing the intellect for *knowledge*, but the teacher who reaches the personality is preparing the pupil for *life;* while the Christian teacher, in going beyond this and reaching the spirituality, is preparing the pupil for *eternity*.

QUESTIONS

1. Prove that God-consciousness is common to man.
2. In what respects do men learn about God through their senses?
3. What is faith?
4. Distinguish between natural and supernatural faith.
5. What is conscience?
6. What evidences of conscience are given in the Old Testament?
7. In what respect does conscience act as a judge?
8. What is the relation of the Bible to conscience?
9. How does environment affect conscience?
10. What is prayer?
11. State three facts that prove the importance of prayer.
12. Name two sources of instruction in prayer.
13. What practice in public prayer should be encouraged?
14. What objectives should be attained when the teacher reaches the mentality and proceeds in an orderly manner?

Part II: *The Teacher*

4

Personality

I. THE INFLUENCE OF PERSONALITY

OUR PERSONALITY is such that we either influence, or are influenced by, everyone with whom we come in contact. One is either marked by, or puts a mark on, every person he meets.

As Miss L. Flora Plummer states it, "Whenever we break through the conventionality which we are prone to use for protection, and enter into the inner circle of the heart of a friend, associate, or companion, we become infected with the perfume, or taint, in the atmosphere of his personality." [1] Because teaching, unlike preaching, is a personal relation and involves the close association of instructor and pupil, the teacher should be:

1. A strong personality

"Teaching," says Edward Thring, "is the communication of life from the living to the living." It is this influencing of life that makes personality such an important pedagogical requisite. "The teacher's life is the life of his teaching." He will teach a little by what he says, more by what he does, but most by what he is. It is this all-important fact that has given point to the oft-repeated saying, "What you are speaks so loudly that I cannot hear what you say."

[1] Plummer, *Soul-Winning Teacher*, p. 35.

49

2. A Christian personality

When a man surrenders his will to God, he does not lose his personality. While his powers are no longer devoted to impressing his own will on others, they are now bent on the promotion of the will of the One to whom he has surrendered his own leadership. Paul's life was just as forcible after his surrender to Jesus Christ as before. From that hour, for him to live was Christ (Phil. 1:21), and everyone who came in contact with him was electrified by the power of his Christian personality.

A real class will study their teacher. They will break through the bars of conventionality and perhaps discover more about their teacher than he has learned about them. His faith, courage, and convictions will speak infinitely louder than his words. Contact with a personality that is charged with the Spirit of Christ can hardly fail to light the spark of desire in the soul of another for a richer, deeper experience in Godlikeness. When Christ is the only true pattern, His followers are epistles "known and read of all men," and the example of a consistent Christian life counts more toward helping others reach a higher standard than any amount of instruction. And in living a blameless life before his pupils, the teacher will be fully rewarded by their expressions of confidence and loyalty. There is nothing more thrilling than to have a child look up into your eyes with full confidence and trust, or defend your statements against all comers. Such a pupil was one day mentioning something his teacher had said, when someone interrupted him.[2]

"It is not so."

"It is so; my teacher said so."

"But it is not so, nevertheless."

[2] Ibid., p. 39.

"If my teacher said it, it is so; and if it is not so, it is so if my teacher said it."

3. A Christian enthusiast

Some time ago a leading American merchant, who had in his employ many exceptionally successful salesmen, was asked by a magazine to suggest half a dozen of the world's greatest salesmen. To the astonishment of all, he named Paul, Luther, Wesley, Whitefield, Spurgeon, and Moody. "These men were eminently successful as salesmen," he wrote, "because they had implicit faith in the house they represented, and perfect confidence that its goods were absolutely needed by the trade. This inspired them with a courage and enthusiasm in the presentation of their wares that demanded and secured attention, and the house was kept busy filling orders."

The Christian teacher represents the same "house" as these great Christian personalities, and there is the same need today for God's Word that there always has been. Success, however, will rest upon the enthusiasm the teacher has for the task, and this enthusiasm will largely be in proportion to his faith in the great enterprise to which he has been called. He must have:

a. Faith in God

There is no doubt that the Christian teacher believes in God, but how far does his faith go? Does he believe in God as Paul and Luther and Moody? Has he a triumphant, aggressive faith?

b. Faith in the Bible

This was a marked characteristic of Jesus. He had absolute faith in His message. Again and again He said, "It is written," because He believed in what was written. No one is going to be enthusiastic over the Bible unless it is the Word of God, but if the Omnipotent and Omniscient One has written to

man, the marvel and the wonder of that message should stir
the heart of every teacher.

c. Faith in the task

Why are you teaching? Is it to please the superintendent?
Is it because you think it your duty? If that is all, there will
be no enthusiasm for your task. But if God has called you to
it, you may rest assured it is the *one thing* that will give you
most pleasure.

God does not call men promiscuously to service, and if He
has set aside this particular task for you, it is well to remember
that He has no one else in all the world who can accomplish
it as well, and that you are in the center of His will in ful-
filling His purpose for you.

II. THE IMITATION OF PERSONALITY

Bishop Huntington has made a valuable contribution to
Sunday school teachers in his remarkable booklet entitled
Unconscious Tuition.[3] The argument of this experienced author is that the teacher is unconsciously exerting an influence
over the pupil continuously, and therefore should be very
careful that his influence be of the highest character.

One has but to watch a group of young children at play to
be convinced that much of what they are doing is an imitation
of their elders. What are some of the things about the teacher
that the pupil is likely to imitate?

1. Order

Order in a Sunday school begins with an orderly superintendent. Order in a class begins with an orderly teacher.
Recognizing this truth, the teacher who wishes for order must
first of all be orderly. Instead of scolding the pupils, he will
show them by example just what he desires.

[3] McKinney, *Practical Pedagogy in the Sunday School,* p. 53.

2. Reverence

Reverence for sacred things is best taught by example. Instead of telling children they must reverence the name of Jesus, the thoughtful teacher will always pronounce that name in such a way that the children instinctively will realize he reverences it. Instead of telling them how to regulate their voices when engaged in prayer, he will modulate his tones so as to produce a quieting effect upon the pupils. The way he speaks, the way he handles his Bible, will speak volumes about reverence.

3. Practiced teaching

There is a time in the life of adolescents when it is almost impossible by argument to convince the young doubters concerning certain things. They are, however, all eyes, when they see the truth lived. Incarnated in one who teaches it, the effect is powerful. Hence, to get others to believe and to do according to the truths for which the Sunday school stands, due regard must be paid to this trait of imitation.

The realization of these truths, which have such high pedagogical value, should be encouraging to teachers. There are those whose training may have been limited. Others are not fluent in expression. In fact, today there are many teachers who seem to feel that their instruction is having little influence upon their pupils. All these need the reminder that their lives are speaking much louder than their words. There is no limit to what may be done because of the trait of imitation.

III. THE RECOGNITION OF PERSONALITY

I shall never forget two important truths that Dr. David James Burrell, our teacher in homiletics at Princeton Seminary, impressed upon us again and again. First of all, he said,

1. Be yourself

Attention has been called to the fact that personality knows no duplication. How well this has been borne out in history. There was only one Julius Caesar, though the memory of his prestige was so great that for centuries after, the rulers of Rome called themselves Caesars. There was only one Oliver Cromwell, and the commonwealth which he founded ended with the passing of that militant Puritan. There was only one Spurgeon, one Moody, one Billy Sunday, though many have unsuccessfully imitated their methods. God has made every one different from everyone else. That difference can be made an important contribution to our success in life.

While it is true we unconsciously imitate others, if we submerge our own selves in the substitution of other personalities, we will be failures. The second thing is

2. Give yourself

The contribution of personality calls for more than an expression from the mind, or an act of the body. It calls for the concentration of the whole being. Naturally, we do not give ourselves until our contribution has become a part of us. It is only when the things we have learned have been appropriated and applied that we can put our heart and our soul into our task. Happy is the teacher who can say when he has finished his instruction, "I am weary *in* the work, but not *of* it." Teaching is a toilsome process. When it commands all our energy, as well as our thought, it will prove tiring. Perhaps there is nothing more exacting of physical strength and endurance than a competitive game of football, and yet one who has engaged in intercollegiate contests has said that the expenditure of mental and physical energy in the presentation of a lesson could leave him as exhausted as a game of football.

IV. THE TRAINING OF PERSONALITY

Many young people get the impression that personality is a gift, and that there is little which can be done for its improvement. It is true that much is acquired by heritage, and that a personality cannot be duplicated. But childhood and adolescence provide the opportunity for the development, and in adult life the improvement, of personality. The teacher may study himself to discover his weak points, or to improve the desirable qualities that his birth and training have established. This scrutiny is important, but it must be more than simply beholding oneself in a glass. If nothing more, then he "goeth his way, and straightway forgetteth what manner of man he was" (Jas. 1:23, 24). The teacher must see and do, if there is to be improvement.

1. Physical improvement

A person of good physique commands the attention and draws the interest of others. His appearance creates a favorable impression, no matter how disappointing later impressions may be. Therefore, a teacher who can present an attractive appearance has an initial advantage. The matter of dress is important in preparing the way for a favorable hearing. Untidiness of person, or extremes in dress, must be avoided. If a person presents a clean, well-groomed appearance, it gives evidence of a reasonable measure of self-respect. Certainly there is truth in John Wesley's comment: "Cleanliness is next to godliness."

Good health will also improve personality. Without it, the buoyancy of spirit and the evidence of energy so essential to effective work, will very likely be lacking.[4] Many troubles, such as poor discipline, lack of interest in the work, want of

---

[4] Eavey, *Principles of Teaching for Christian Teachers,* p. 82.

sympathy between teacher and pupils, often have their source in the defective physical condition of the teacher. It is most difficult for a teacher who is not well physically to be at his or her best in mental life and spiritual life.

Voice is another factor that discloses the personality. The voice can be improved. The weak voice should be strengthened, and the loud, harsh voice, modulated. The tempo should be studied, so there may at times be rapidity of expression, and at other times pauses for impression. Inflections should be studied, so that a question may be detected before the sentence is completed. The voice is such an important factor in teaching, and has such large possibilities for effectiveness, that every teacher should give some time and thought to voice training.

In classes in observation and practice teaching, the appearance, physical condition, and voice of the teacher are always criticized.

2. Mental improvement

It has already been pointed out, that the teacher must be a learner if he is to share with the pupil in the learning process; but he will have a program of study not merely that he may be informed. This is important, as we shall see in a subsequent chapter. But he will discover that the attention he is giving to intellectual development is also affecting his personality. The teacher who has a well-organized program of study, and adheres to it faithfully, will become mentally alert, which is one of the most essential requirements for attaining that place in teaching to which every ambitious instructor should aspire.

3. Spiritual improvement

Character itself does not make anyone a Christian.[5] This is the work of God. But a Christian, and especially a Christian teacher, because of his greater influence by way of example,

[5] Eavey, *op. cit.,* p. 89.

must be a person of the highest moral standards. Impurity, compromise with wrong, indulgence in questionable practices, will have to be abandoned. The Christian teacher must "abstain from all appearance of evil" (I Thess. 5:22). The Christian teacher will walk circumspectly through the maze of this world's evils. He will ever recognize that his "citizenship is in heaven." His life will be so permeated with the purpose to do the will of God that for him to live will mean occupation with spiritual and not with material things. As a teacher, his supreme desire will be to give his life unreservedly in service, sacrifice, and interceding prayer, for the eternal destiny of pupils whom God has entrusted to his care.

It might be well, in conclusion, to point out that there is a danger of giving too much attention to *our* personalities. There is always a danger of losing ourselves through the imitation of others. Our personality will develop, not by measurement on a comparative scale, or by morbid self-analysis. Rather should we subject ourselves to a searching scrutiny when we fail, or when we succeed. This will reveal points of weakness and of strength, as well as the clues to those things we should set about to improve. Life at its best must be the ideal of the teacher. It is the teacher's life, first of all, to which the pupil will look. And the teacher who is striving for life at its best will more and more embody those traits which he would wish to develop in his pupils. If we look to the things we do, the thoughts we think, and the character we express, our personalities will take care of themselves.

QUESTIONS

1. Name the three important characteristics of the Christian teacher.
2. How does the teacher instruct by his life?

3. Why would some eminent church leaders be most successful salesmen?
4. What three traits will mark a Christian enthusiast?
5. Name three things about a teacher that the pupil is likely to imitate.
6. In what two ways can a personality be recognized?
7. What does physique have to do with a personality?
8. How will good health improve personality?
9. In what respects does the voice affect the personality?
10. How is the personality affected through intellectual development?
11. Why are the highest moral standards necessary for a Christian teacher?
12. What is the danger of giving too much attention to our personality?

5

Preparation

ONE of the greatest tragedies of the Protestant church is that so little attention has been given to the preparation of its teachers. Perhaps this has been due to the larger place, in modern times, accorded the pastor and the evangelist. But if we study the program in the apostolic church, we shall discover that while the evangelist founded the church, and the pastor shepherded, or governed the church, it was the teacher who edified, or built up, the church. Nothing can do more to encourage a better preparation for the teaching ministry than a reminder of

I. THE IMPORTANCE OF TEACHING

In considering the importance of the teacher, we need, first of all, to recognize his

1. Value to the Sunday school

No matter how large or how well organized a Sunday school may be, it will always pivot around the educational triad—the teacher, the lesson, and the class. Of these, the first and most important factor is the teacher. In fact, the teacher stands as the central factor in the whole Sunday school program. Marion Lawrance said, "The teacher is the highest and most important officer in the Sunday school." Some superintendents will object to this statement, but nevertheless it is true. Only in an executive capacity does the superintendent outrank the teacher. The office of superintendent, like that of the school principal, is to promote and to protect the all-important work of teaching. Good teachers make a good Sunday school, and the superintendent who gives his first and foremost attention to the selection and training of a teaching staff, eventually will be at the head of a successful Sunday school. Emerson said, "Let me select the teacher, and I care not who arranges the course of study." The president of one of our great universities says that "eighty-five per cent of a college education depends upon the teacher, and not more than fifteen per cent upon the curriculum." The teacher, therefore, is the supreme factor in any school. It is well for superintendents to recognize that the teacher is the key to

a. Sunday school enlargement

How does the Sunday school grow? Not by contests. These may provide a temporary increase in numbers, but the net results are so small as to be practically worthless. Nor can we build up our Sunday school by a system of rewards. We cannot pay children for going to Sunday school. This is an unprofitable financial expenditure, and an improper plan for winning their interest and devotion. The teacher is the key to Sunday school expansion. We cannot possibly have more pupils until we have more teachers. Crowding the classes of incompetent teachers will never build up the Sunday school. Before a superintendent should undertake a canvass of the neighborhood, he should set in motion those agencies that would assure him of the necessary teaching staff to take care of the anticipated increased enrollment. To double attendance, one must first of all double the teaching staff. This is so obvious that it might as well be regarded as an axiom or law.

b. Sunday school improvement

The teacher is the key not only to Sunday school enlargement, but also to Sunday school improvement. Take the matter of attendance. None of our Protestant denominations are able to even approximate the records of our public schools. In fact, there are only too many instances where the attendance is not much better than one-half of the enrollment.

Lack of punctuality is equally distressing. We find that our failure to achieve punctuality in Sunday school is reflected in the late comers for church services. Protestantism presents no more pathetic picture to unbelievers than the half-filled pews and tardy attendance, that are only too apparent in many of our churches, Sunday after Sunday.

These failures are largely due to inefficient teaching. A real teacher will create sufficient interest not only to command regular attendance, but also punctuality. While the Sunday school can assist in these matters by keeping records and encouraging real accomplishment on the part of the pupil, nothing can take the place of the teacher in commanding the interest of the pupil.

Then there is the matter of discipline. Disorder in any Sunday school is a teaching problem. When pupils are really interested, disorder vanishes. The pupils cannot be interested if they have an untrained and unprepared teacher.

2. Value to the pupil

But valuable as the teacher is to the Sunday school, he is even more important to the pupil. It is the pupil's contact with life and not his contact with books which most powerfully affects his own life.

I wonder how many have been impressed in reading Paul's farewell to the elders at Ephesus (Acts 20:17–38). I can hardly reread this familiar passage without tears coming to my eyes. Paul had been their beloved teacher for three years. During this time, he says, "I kept back nothing that was profitable unto you, but have showed you, and have taught you publicly, and from house to house" (v. 20). "I have coveted no man's silver, or gold, or apparel. Yea, ye yourselves know, that these hands have ministered unto my necessities, and to them that were with me. I have showed you all things, how that so labouring ye ought to support the weak, and to remember the words of the Lord Jesus, how he said, It is more blessed to give than to receive" (vv. 33–35).

It was not so much what Paul taught as what he demonstrated in his own life that seems to have impressed these Ephesians. His class had learned to love their teacher. Now look at the final scene. He kneels down and prays with them all. And then, we read, "they all wept sore, and fell on Paul's neck, and kissed him" (v. 37). How they loved their teacher! They were not thinking so much of what he had taught, but that they would see his face no more. His departure meant that something well-nigh indispensable had gone out of their lives. Such is the teacher's influence upon his pupils.

It takes a $50,000-a-year man to guide a client, develop a gold mine, or put a corporation on its feet. Of how much more worth is a Sunday school teacher who takes that unpromising boy, guides him, develops him, puts him on his feet and makes a man of him.

My father was a Presbyterian minister. During his ministry, covering many years, he organized eleven churches, erected four church buildings, and contributed many articles to the religious press. His greatest work, however, came in the sunset days, when he could no longer preach. He gathered the boys of the village in his home and taught them. Three of his boys became Christian doctors, seven, successful Christian business men. Others in his class became Christian ministers. As a matter of fact, no less than seventeen young men who had sat under his instruction were eventually to devote their lives to fulltime Christian service.

On the tomb of that great Chinese teacher, Confucius, there is this epitaph: "He teaches for ten thousand years." On the tomb of every consecrated Sunday school teacher might well be written, "He teaches for eternity."

II. BASIC TRAINING

If the Sunday school teacher's work is of such great importance, why should he not receive the same adequate preparation for his task as our pastors and our evangelists? While the teacher may be denied recognition and remuneration, surely we cannot deprive him of training. We believe and insist upon Spirit-filled teachers, but can we hope that the Holy Spirit will honor unnecessary and unwarranted ignorance? As teachers we are only instruments upon which the Holy Spirit must play, but surely it will make a difference whether the instrument is in tune or not. A celebrated pianist cannot afford to ruin his reputation by playing on an instrument that has not been prepared for his touch. If our teachers are to be tuned instruments for God's use, ought they not to be prepared? We want Spirit-filled teachers, but the Holy Spirit is not honored by our ignorance or by our indolence. It often has been said that teachers are born and not made. The statement represents a half-truth. Teachers are born, but, as someone has remarked, they are not born *made*. Heredity makes a contribution to every life. It gives the start, the potentialities which can become realities, and its contribution can be neutralized or improved by environment. Often what is regarded as a natural gift is in reality an acquired habit. The success of any teacher is in a large degree dependent upon his enthusiasm for his task, his love for his pupils, and his thoroughness in preparation.[1] No successful teacher is under any delusion as to the value of good hard work as a necessity for making the most of whatever helpful contributions have been made by heredity and environment.

[1] Eavey, *Principles of Teaching for Christian Teachers*, p. 18.

When we appreciate the office of teacher, we shall come to appreciate the need of preparation. Christ was thirty years preparing for three years of public life. The doctor, the lawyer, or the professional man, spends years in hard study and application, that he may be efficient when the crucial moment arises. It will not do to be obliged to consult a book when the artery is severed and the lifeblood is flowing away. Somebody must "know how," or a life will be lost. Let an unskilled surgeon bungle his work, and a child may become a cripple for life. Such a mistake is a tragedy, but not so serious as the blunder of a teacher who ministers to an immortal soul. Surely the Lord can use to better advantage teachers who are thoroughly equipped for their work than those who are not. The Sunday school period at best is all too brief. How essential then that every diamond minute of every golden hour be turned to the best possible account. Only the trained teacher can utilize these precious moments to the best advantage. In order to do so, again and again there must be a reminder of

1. The importance of training

a. Gives prestige to the Sunday school

Our Christian colleges are presenting themselves to the public as real schools. They issue annual catalogs, listing the members of their faculties, with the degree of preparation each possesses for his work. They provide evidence of being real schools by noting that they have real teachers on the faculty. If the Sunday school is to demonstrate that it is an educational institution, where all-important instruction in the Bible may be acquired, we must raise the standard of our teaching requirements. Are we not approaching the day when we shall have the same training requirements for our Sunday school teachers as we have for our public school teachers? Shall we not gain the respect of thousands, who now have little or no interest in the Sunday school, when it becomes known that we consider the Bible a study of sufficient importance as to require trained men and women to teach it? Are mathematics, history, and science so much more important than the Bible that we require only trained men and women to teach them? How can we justify the training of our pastors and utterly neglect the teachers in the Sunday school? Surely no one will think that the interval of time necessary to pass from the Bible class to a lively group of boys would be sufficient to transform an auditor into a well-trained teacher. Why should the superintendent ask some inexperienced, untrained member of the Bible class if he will teach? Why should he teach? How can he? Instead of the entreating inquiry, "Will you teach?" would it not be better to put the question, "Can you teach?"

b. Gives confidence to the teacher

Not only does a faculty of trained teachers give prestige to the Sunday school, but it also gives confidence to the teacher. What makes teaching a pleasure? Why should the preparation of a Sunday school lesson ever be considered drudgery? Well, we only dread it and make hard work of it because we are not trained. A skilled musician does not find playing upon the piano drudgery. He so thoroughly enjoys it that it is hard to keep him away from the instrument. A good cook will enjoy the time she spends in the kitchen. A skilled player will not need to be coaxed to play baseball. We enjoy being engaged in the things which we can do easily or well.

Did it ever occur to you that this is exactly the position of the trained teacher? The trained teacher approaches the study of each week's lesson with confidence, not only on the basis of knowledge secured through time spent in training, but also in the realization that the task of preparing this particular lesson will be greatly simplified because of previous knowledge he has gained. The trained teacher is able to bring the study of many months, if not many years, to bear upon the preparation and presentation of a single lesson.

c. Gives confidence to the pupil

What is it that enables us to win and hold the respect of our pupils? As has already been pointed out, they will respect us primarily for what we *are,* but at the same time we must not overlook the fact that they will also be influenced by what we *know.* Our pupils will admire and follow us because they are convinced that we know what we are talking about. We not only know, but we know that we know.

The Christian teacher who is unprepared for his task is at a tremendous disadvantage. How can a boy or girl who attends public school five days a week, and gets the very best instruction from a well-trained teacher, have much respect for an untrained or poorly prepared teacher, under whom he or she sits for only one hour a week! How much value is such a boy likely to attach to that which the Sunday school teacher is supposed to be teaching? Any normal boy or girl is as certain to make comparison between the work done in public school and that done at Sunday school, as he is prone to compare horse and buggy with the modern automobile.

The public school teacher may be a man of opinion, but the Sunday school teacher must be a man of conviction. Who may hope to sway this indifferent and disinterested world unless he can teach with conviction? This is a great day for opinion, and how divergent the views they express! What we need greatly is conviction. Few, if any, have died for an opinion. Thousands have died for a conviction. The secular teacher may call eternity "a great perhaps," but no one wants to live or die for "a great perhaps." Eternity is the Sunday school teacher's certainty, because his Redeemer liveth! It is the Sunday school teacher's assurance of his many-mansioned home.

BIBLE

It is the Sunday school teacher's confidence of receiving the Master's "Well done," that may be counted upon to shape a life and mold a destiny.

No pupil will have confidence in a Sunday school teac'' who does not know the Word of God. Only insofar as H₊ mastered the Textbook is he in position to create conf that the words he speaks are of far greater significanc all the words of all the teachers in the institutions of education in the world.

2. The content of training

What constitutes a course in teacher training? T .re four factors: the textbook, the pupil, the teaching, ̣ the school.

a. The Bible

It is absolutely necessary that the teacher be familiar with the textbook he teaches. No one ventures to teach fractions or decimals until he has mastered arithmetic. No one is able to teach a single chapter of the Bible to advantage until he has a knowledge of the sixty-six books. To teach intelligently and practically, any portion of a subject, the instructor should be familiar with the whole. One is amazed to find so many Christian teachers who do not appear anxious to master the world's greatest Book.

Professor William Lyon Phelps, for many years head of the department of English literature, Yale University, made a statement that was widely broadcast. This scholar, familiar as he was with all literature, declared that a knowledge of the Bible was essential if a man was to be considered educated. He said, "Everyone who has a knowledge of the Bible may truly be called educated; and no other learning or culture, no matter how extensive or elegant, can among Europeans and Americans form a proper substitute. I thoroughly believe in a university education for both men and women, but I believe the knowledge of the Bible is more valuable than a college course without a knowledge of the Bible."

There is no problem of human life upon which the Bible does not throw light. There is no moral or spiritual difficulty concerning which it does not provide direction. There are no questions as to the life here or hereafter for which it does not furnish the required help to arrive at a satisfactory answer. Its materials are so rich and varied that the needs of every age level are adequately met by it. It is enough to satisfy the inquiring mind of a little child, the questioning mind of the older child, the disturbed mind of the restless youth, and the hungry mind of the young adult. The teacher who has assimilated the truths of the Bible and has relived the experiences which it so faithfully and vividly records, has an inexhaustible source of living water to be shared with those whom he would teach.

b. Related subjects

In addition to a thorough knowledge of the textbook, the teacher should be familiar with related subjects.

(1). Geography

Children of school age should be as well posted on the geography of Bible lands as on that of their own country. New interest is added when pupils can visualize the mountains, rivers, and towns of Palestine, but what the pupil would learn, the teacher must first know.

(2). History

Boys and girls studying ancient history at school will be surprised and pleased to discover that their teacher is well informed on the events and characters that parallel the narratives of the Bible. Tourists spend much time visiting historical landmarks, and sentiment may be developed in the heart of the Bible student as he becomes familiar with the history of the places in Palestine which have been immortalized by the journeys of the Lord Jesus Christ.

(3). *Antiquities*

The life and customs of the ancients differ widely from our own. A knowledge of them is essential for establishing a comprehensive setting for every Bible scene.

c. *The pupil*

The Bible should not be studied apart from human life. Indeed, a chief source of Bible interest and power is in its portrayal of living men and women. They serve as a mirror in which we see ourselves and others. He who would teach the Bible must know and love people. To know and love people is not an easy assignment. There is a science of human nature that is just beginning to unfold. Teachers are coming to realize that the study of those whom they would teach requires time and techniques, no less than the study of the subject which they would teach. Next to the Bible itself, fascinating and rewarding will be systematic study of the individuals who constitute a given Sunday school class.

A grammar school teacher once made this boast: "If I had my hands tied behind my back, and my eyes blindfolded, I could still teach the pupils of my grade, and preserve discipline." She had been teaching this age group for so many years that she believed she was thoroughly acquainted with all their peculiarities. There was no trick they could play, no device they could put into operation, with which they could catch her off guard.

Boys and girls often are better students of human nature than their teachers. They may not always get their lessons, but they also may study their teacher sufficiently to know just when they will be called upon to recite. We must study the child as he studies us, for only in that way can we ever hope to find an entrance into his life. "The child mind," says Patterson Dubois, "is a citadel that can be taken neither by stealth nor by storm, but there is a natural way of approach and a gate of easy entry always open to him who knows how to find it."

d. The technique of teaching

No textbook, however well prepared, will ever supersede the alert teacher. The radio and moving pictures are effective agencies in imparting information, but they will ever be subordinate to the living teacher. A successful pastor is credited with this statement: "Few pastors have been privileged to be assisted by a more consecrated group of teachers than has been my lot. Many of them had taken courses by correspondence and were exceptionally well informed as to the contents of the Bible, but their consecration and knowledge of the Bible were not sufficient. They still needed the technique of teaching to enable them to gain and hold the interest of their pupils."

e. Sunday school administration

Mark Hopkins needed only a log to equip his school, but most teachers require proper surroundings to enable them to do their best work. Knowledge of administration is essential that the Sunday school may carry out its God-given mission. This study best serves its purpose when it instructs superintendents that their major responsibility is to protect and promote the teaching ministry.

III. PERENNIAL TRAINING

The successful teacher will never cease to be a student. He must continually grow in knowledge and in teaching power. The completion of a training course will be the beginning of a program that will keep him fully prepared for his task. We recall that Dr. Thomas Arnold was asked why he found it necessary to prepare for each day's lesson. He gave this memorable reply: "I would rather that my pupils would drink from a running stream than from a stagnant pool." In order that teaching may be a delight rather than a drudgery, it is important that the teacher be kept in training for his task. An athlete must constantly exercise. A musician must practice daily to be at his best. Likewise a teacher will find his class a satisfying pleasure if he gives attention to

1. Bible study

No course in teacher training can ever provide enough time for the mastery of the Bible. At best it can provide us only with an outline of the outstanding facts, leaving the details to be filled in by subsequent study. Dr. Gaines S. Dobbins, says, "It is worth all its costs to acquire a working mastery of the whole Bible." [2] There are teachers who teach "from hand to mouth"—that is, from one lesson to the next, as if there were little or no connection. Others teach out of the overflow —that is, from a fullness of knowledge of the total context. No argument is needed to prove the superiority of the teacher who possesses a rich background of general Bible knowledge.

Perhaps no other book is so mistreated as the Bible, even by those who love it. Day after day it may be neglected, sometimes practically discarded in favor of a periodical containing "helps" for a limited set of lessons. More often it is used only for the study of a given lesson, without reference to what goes before or to what follows. What hope is there for Bible mastery without systematic study? There are various methods that can be employed. But method, or no method, teachers should constantly read the Bible. Dr. G. Campbell Morgan once asked an audience, "If you read the Bible an hour a day in the morning, while you are fresh, in how many hours

[2] Dobbins, *The Improvement of Teaching in the Sunday School,* p. 14.

would you read it through?" Guesses ran as high as five hundred. "But the answer," said Dr. Morgan, "is sixty hours." [3]

The late Dr. John R. Sampey, of the Southern Baptist Theo-
logical Seminary, proposed an interesting plan for the reading of the Bible. He suggested three bookmarks; one for
Genesis and the books that follow; one for Job and the books
that follow, and one for the New Testament. Then read a
chapter a day, but read in every section. Devoting a minimum
of 15 minutes a day to this reading, the teacher will cover
every chapter of the Bible in 520 days, or about 18 months.
The total time required will be approximately 130 hours. The
advantages of such a plan are many. A balanced diet is afforded. Interest is sustained. While the Old Testament is
being read through once, the New Testament will be read
twice. The Old Testament and the New Testament will thus
be kept vitally related. In the course of the years, the persistent
reader will secure a grasp of the whole Bible that will im-
measurably enrich his teaching. [4]

I would add a suggestion to Dr. Sampey's plan. Where it
is possible to have both morning and evening devotions, let
the morning be given to the Old Testament, and the evening
to the New. The Old Testament readings will alternate between the legal and the historical books, and the poetical and
prophetical portion. New Testament interest can be increased
if, instead of reading the Gospels one after another, the following plan is observed:

Books	Chapters
Matthew	
I and II Corinthians	63
Galatians	

[3] Dobbins, *op. cit.,* p. 42.
[4] Dobbins, *op. cit.,* p. 43.

Mark Ephesians Philippians Colossians I and II Thessalonians I and II Timothy Titus Philemon Hebrews	65

Luke
Acts of the Apostles
    (As Luke wrote both the Gospel
    and the Acts, these books should be
    read in succession.)
Romans
	68

John General Epistles Revelation	64

This plan lends variety and associates the author with all his writings.

2. Pupil study

Courses in pupil study are not sufficient to provide instruction concerning an individual. No description in a book ever fits the particular problem with which the teacher is wrestling in the form of a Billy Johnson or a George Brown. The books on child nature can help one to know principles and laws, but beyond this the successful teacher will have to study his own particular pupils in order to deal successfully with them. The teacher will not only have to become child-minded, but person-minded. He will soon find himself watching each member of the class with keen interest, listening to conversations that reveal unexpected meanings, observing actions that portray hitherto unknown aspects of character. As the teacher comes to know and to love his class, to understand and to appreciate each individual more fully, he will find that his task has become a source of increased satisfaction, and one that is fruitful in results.

3. Study period

Certain hours should be set aside each week for the preparation of the lesson. This time should be recognized as sacred, and nothing should be permitted to interfere with it. This God-given task is far too important for its preparation to be relegated to the spare moments that are left after matters of comparatively little consequence have received attention. If possible, a secluded spot should be sought, and no interruptions tolerated until the work is completed.

There must be system in the preparation, as well as in the presentation, of the lesson. Teachers who have an orderly plan of procedure in working out their lessons will be able to accomplish nearly twice as much in a given period of time. Suggestions along this line will be given in the chapters on the preparation of the lesson (12 and 13).

Perennial training will not only require constant study of the Bible and of the individual pupils that compose the class, but also

4. Personal attention

a. Physically fit

No teacher can over-do all week and come to class on Sunday with energy and enthusiasm. Instead of keeping late hours Saturday evening, the teacher's Sunday (Lord's Day) should begin at sunset the night before, that on the morrow he may assume his all-important task in the best possible physical condition.

b. Mentally alert

A good teacher, like a good preacher, will read constantly, systematically, and intelligently. At least one good book along his line of study should be read each quarter, and it would be to his advantage to subscribe for several Sunday school periodicals. He will do well if he reads more, but he should not read more than he can digest. One should not read without thinking, and should not think without writing. It is well to have a notebook handy in which can be entered not only that which every teacher should know, but that which he can use for some specific lesson or can prescribe for the peculiar needs of a pupil.

c. Spiritually alive

It is not enough to study the Bible in order to meet the needs of others. There must be a personal ministry to our own spiritual requirements. It is the teacher's fidelity to his daily devotions that enables him to present his instruction forcibly. Teacher, keep ever in prayer, if you would have the power to be quiet and to be masterful under the most trying circumstances. It is only those who keep in fellowship with God who have the poise which is so essential to the Sunday school teacher.

QUESTIONS

1. In what two ways is the teacher important to the Sunday school?
2. What about Paul's teaching impressed the Ephesians most?
3. Upon what does success of any teacher largely depend?
4. Give three reasons why teacher training is important.
5. How does the trained teacher give prestige to the Sunday school?
6. Why does a trained teacher approach his task with confidence?
7. What effect does the trained teacher have upon the attitude of the pupils?
8. What four factors are involved in teacher training?

9. Why is a knowledge of the Bible the most important requisite for successful Christian teaching?

10. What are three subjects related to the Bible with which the teacher should be familiar?

11. Why is pupil study important in preparation of the teacher?

12. How can teaching be improved by a plan of Bible study?

13. Give Dr. Sampey's suggestion for reading the Bible in 520 days.

14. Why is a study period important?

15. Make three suggestions for the personal attention of the teacher.

6

Aims

WE read in Scripture of seven hundred lefthanded men of the tribe of Benjamin who were experts in the use of a sling (Judg. 20:16). By constant practice these warriors had learned to co-ordinate so perfectly the use of their eye and hand that "every one could sling stones at an hair-breadth, and not miss." But the marvel of that wonderful skill was not so much in the masterly throw as in the perfect aim. These men had learned to fix their eyes on the object they wished to hit, and to keep them there until the stone went straight to its mark.

It is necessary that the Christian teacher have a definite aim or objective. It is true there is hardly another school in which more work without aim or plan is done than in the Sunday school. Sometimes this is due to the old lesson system of the Sunday school, and its treatment, which is lacking in definite aims. Sometimes it is the pastor or superintendent who is responsible for the curriculum. Especially, however, it is the individual teachers, who are destitute of an aim. A teacher without an aim is like a ship floundering in the ocean without a compass and without direction. He is flung hither and thither, as the wind of fancy, of a lesson, a book, an experience, or of ordinary laziness, may drive him. Work of such nature will hardly satisfy in the end. There is no joy, no inspiration about it. Aimlessness in teaching also produces restless and indifferent pupils. Pupils in the hands of aimless teachers neither learn how to understand the detail, nor how to unite it with the whole. Under the best circumstances, what they gain are fragmentary, interrupted, disjointed, piecemeal perceptions. They neither perceive anything of the unity of the Bible and the divine plan of redemption which God has followed for their salvation, nor of the unity of the way of salvation which they must follow.

I. IMPORTANCE OF AN AIM

The Sunday school teacher must have a clear and well-defined aim, and hold tenaciously to it until its accomplishment can be fully realized. Before a teacher can use principles and methods aright, he must have clearly and adequately in mind the ends to be attained. The better he knows where he is going, the more intelligently he can and will provide the means for getting there. Being sure of the aim of his endeavors, he can make good use of his knowledge of truth, pupils, principles, and methods in the direction of that aim. Learning is never actively engaged in for its own sake; it is always a means to an end. The clearer the conceptions of that end, the better can the means be chosen for the realization of it. Much can be said about the importance of a right aim in teaching, but at least three very good reasons should be designated.

1. Gives direction and destination

Aim gives direction to thought, activity, and the processes necessary for effecting desirable changes. Teaching with an aim implies that the teacher has thought through with a definite purpose in view, both his own activity and the probable activity of his pupils. He has worked out a careful plan, determined upon a starting point, considered the successive steps along the way, and decided upon a destination. This aim may be for a series of lessons, but it should be kept sight of in the presentation of a single lesson. As a consequence of such aiming, the entire teaching situation is enriched, and the pupils reap the results in terms of realization of the true outcomes of effective education.

2. Determines progress

Aim makes possible the measurement of progress. When we know where we are going and the way we are going, we can measure from week to week the advance that has been made. An aim also provides the knowledge by which to determine how effectively the desirable activities have been performed. Do results show that we have persistently kept to our purpose? Without a clear aim, there is no basis for measurement.

3. Provides courage and confidence

A right aim inspires the worker. "Nothing succeeds so well as success," and no success brings such a thrill as results from earnest effort directed toward the attainment of a high and lofty end. As the mountain climber keeps his eyes turned toward the peak he purposes to conquer, he has the heart to pass through the intervening valleys, and to climb the lower elevations he meets on the way. So the teacher, with his gaze fixed on a distant aim, has courage and energy in the face of great obstacles to press on, until final success crowns his efforts.

II. SOME SUGGESTED AIMS

What should constitute a clear and well-defined aim for the Christian teacher?

1. Dean Goodrich C. White says that it should include a threefold purpose:

   a. To lead each pupil to a knowledge of God's will.

b. To lead each pupil to an acceptance of Jesus Christ as personal Saviour and Lord.

c. To develop a Christian character, which will be expressed through worship, right living, and efficient service.[1]

2. Dr. H. E. Carmack puts it this way:

a. Bring the pupil to Christ.

b. Build him up in Christ.

c. Send him forth to work for Christ.[2]

Dr. Theodore Schmauk adds a line which we heartily endorse: "The aim of the teacher is to make the Word of God clear and cogent." [3] To teacher and pupil alike it is of greater consequence to know just what the Bible says than any implied inference of what it may teach.

In order that the Christian teacher may not lose himself and go drifting among the speculative and so-called "practical" issues of the day, it is imperative that his aim be closely allied to the study and use of the Bible. There is an opinion afloat that the exclusive aim of the teacher is to produce right living. We are told that it matters little what a child is taught, so long as he is brought to act correctly. Instead of "in the nurture and admonition of the Lord," the new education aims to bring up children by "development and expression." It is not what a boy likes, nor what he feels he needs, that is to be the teacher's chief concern. Only the truth revealed in the Bible has power to transform life and establish Christian character, therefore it is of the greatest importance that the aim of the teacher be governed by knowledge of, and instruction in, the Word of God.

3. According to Dr. M. Reu, the aim of Christian education is:

a. Faithfully to impart and anchor in the intellect of the

---

[1] G. C. White, *Teaching in the Sunday School,* p. 170.
[2] Carmack, *How to Teach a Sunday School Lesson,* p. 14.
[3] Schmauk, *How to Teach in Sunday School,* p. 45.

*rising generations all the holy truths upon which the life of
the mature congregation fundamentally is based.*

b. To stir their emotions to a vital interest in these truths.

*c. To bend the will so it may run in the paths in which
the Holy Spirit in His own time and hour lifts them into
personal faith.*

"If I should express it in simple and plain, and at the same
time in the most comprehensible and easily retainable way,"
he says, "I would say, we are to reveal God to our pupils." [4]

4. Dr. C. E. Eavey contends that the perfect man of God
is the inclusive aim. He says:

"A Christian teacher is a human being who has been made a
new creature in Christ Jesus. His absorbing purpose is to glorify
God; this is the end in view for his life. His teaching and all that
he does is the direction of activity for the attainment of this end.
To him, the Bible is the inspired Word of God, and, with intelligent conviction, he turns to it to find an inclusive aim for
his teaching. As a teacher, he has aims subordinate to his inclusive aim as a Christian, that is, to glorify God. But as a teacher
again, he has one inclusive aim, which, in turn, has within it
subordinate aims. The practical question which remains after all
that has been heretofore expressed is put together, is: What is a
clear and definite aim for Christian teaching that is sufficiently
inclusive for all other aims to be subordinated to it? The direct
answer to this question is, The inclusive aim of the Christian
teacher is 'that the man of God may be perfect, throughly furnished unto all good works' (II Tim. 3:17). All of Christian
teaching is directed to the one final and only aim of the upbuild-
ing of those taught in perfection of godly character." [5]

III. CHRIST'S AIM FOR HIS DISCIPLES

In determining the aim for the Christian teacher, nothing
can be of greater assistance than the study of our Lord's ob-

[4] Reu, *How to Teach in a Sunday School,* p. 158.
[5] Eavey, *Principles of Teaching for Christian Teachers,* p. 54.

jectives in connection with His training class. He was the
master of all teachers, and the master of all teaching. Sixty
out of ninety times that He was addressed, He was called
Teacher, and His students were called disciples, or learners.
Again and again they called Him Teacher. What was the
supreme purpose of His instruction? Obviously the answer
cannot be found outside of the Gospels. A careful examination of the writings of the four evangelists, who so marvelously agreed in their accounts of our Lord's life and death,
will reveal the following objectives of the Master-Teacher.

1. To reveal God's gracious and glorious plan for His
disciples.

He declared, "I am come that they might have life, and
that they might have it more abundantly" (John 10:10).
"Fear not, little flock; for it is your Father's good pleasure to
give you the kingdom" (Luke 12:32).

The life which He brought and of which He taught was
eternal, not temporal. He did not seek to impress His disciples
with the benefits of civilization, or wealth, or the cultivation
of arts or science. Because eternity is infinitely more than time,
our Lord did not consider it worth while to discuss the temporal reforms which loom so conspicuously on the horizon. This
life, with all of its questions and interests, is so relatively un-
important compared to the eternal program outlined to His
disciples that repeatedly He was led to ask those unanswerable
questions, "What shall it profit a man, if he shall gain the
whole world, and lose his own soul? Or what shall a man
give in exchange for his soul?" (Mark 8:36, 37).

The life which He brought and of which He taught was
spiritual rather than material. It was not the aim of Christ to
secure better legislation in order to improve the condition of
the laborer, as many of our social workers today would have
us believe. He did not seek to have His disciples elected to

worldly positions so that they might have wholesome influence with men. More than that, He did not even promise His faithful followers so much as an existence worthy of man, with indemnity in case of death, disease, old age, and invalidity. Why? Because the soul is infinitely more than the body, and the kingdom of heaven infinitely more than the kingdoms of earth. He constantly fixed their attention on the infinitely more important things. In this world they would suffer hunger, imprisonment, persecution, martyrdom (Matt. 10:16–28), but in all this they were to rejoice and be exceeding glad, for great was their reward in heaven (Matt. 5:10–12).

2. To win them to active faith in Himself as Saviour and King.

God's offer of the more abundant life was dependent on the acceptance of His beloved Son, who came to die for their salvation (John 3:16). That this was one of the great objectives of Jesus' teaching is shown by the importance He attached to Peter's confession (Matt. 16:16), saying that upon that rock He would build His Church. He made it plain that His coming into the world was for the purpose of accomplishing God's will (John 6:38), and that to do God's will men must believe on Him (John 6:29, 40).

And not only did Christ seek to win people to faith in Himself as Saviour, but also as King. He would have them believe that He was the promised Messiah (John 4:25, 26) and the coming King, of whose glorious reign the Old Testament prophets wrote. He spoke parable after parable about the kingdom of which He was the King.

3. To prepare and train His disciples to be His witnesses.

This was clearly stated in the first call to His disciples—"Follow me, and I will make you fishers of men" (Matt. 4:19). To this end He sent them out to teach and evangelize under His oversight (Matt. 10:5–15), conducting, as it were, a practical work department for His teacher training class. That this was the climax of all the other objectives of His ministry is evident from the great commission, in which He gave final instructions to His disciples, to go and teach all people (Matt. 28:19). And it must be pointed out that the training and commission of the disciples were for the purpose of evangelizing rather than converting the world. This is clearly evident from the fuller explanation of the divine program as it is given in Acts 15:14–17, and from the methods of the apostolic Church, that practically evangelized the civilized world (the Roman Empire) in that day (Rom. 15:19–24).

Notice how closely the Master-Teacher adhered to His objectives in His teaching. When the young materialist requested that He act as judge of an estate and direct an equitable division of wealth, Christ told the story of the rich fool to impress the fact that a man's life consisteth not in the abundance of things which he possesseth (Luke 12:13–21). When criticism was made because the alabaster box of expensive ointment was poured on His head instead of the money being given to the poor, our Lord called attention to the fact that this act was a testimony of faith that He was the appointed Saviour of mankind (Mark 14:3–9). When asked to rebuke His disciples because they prepared for Him a royal entry into Jerusalem and acknowledged Him as King, He declared that if they were silent the stones would cry out His imperial prerogatives (Luke 19:35–40). When the mother of two of His disciples asked that they be given the highest offices in His kingdom, He taught them that like Himself they were called to be ministers rather than rulers (Matt. 20:20–28). When after His resurrection it was suggested that the time had come for Him to restore again the kingdom to Israel, He declared that the divine program was for the disciples to be His witnesses unto the uttermost parts of the earth (Acts 1: 6–8).

IV. APPLICATION OF CHRIST'S AIM

Having observed the great objectives of our Lord's teaching, and His close adherence to them, let us now apply them to the aim of Christian teachers. While this subject will be taken up again, when we discuss the application of instruction (Lesson 15), it is well to introduce it at this time. As a result of this study, may we not say that the aim of the Christian teacher is *to shape the immortal destiny of a soul according to the Word of God?* And in order to do this, the Christian teacher must:

1. Reveal God's gracious and glorious purpose for His children

The more abundant life of which Christ taught His disciples, is the same marvelous theme of the Christian teacher. Truly, "eye hath not seen, nor ear heard, neither have entered into the heart of man, the things which God hath prepared for them that love him" (I Cor. 2:9). Scripture and science testify to the fact that the greatness of God is unsearchable (Ps. 145:3). Modern astronomy reveals a universe of countless orbs in which the earth is but a speck and the sun a spark. And as if this immensity were not enough, there are an indeterminable number of other universes as vast and incomprehensible as our own. But the privilege of the Christian teacher is to reveal the God whose "greatness is unsearchable," and His gracious and glorious purpose for His children. From the Bible and the Bible alone we learn of the interest of the mighty and majestic God in this earth, though it be but a grain in the mountain of creation, and of His great love for the hopeless and helpless people upon it. Before one can teach he must have a real conception of the priceless value of one immortal soul, and a vision of the far-reaching happiness that is the portion of every child of God.

2. Lead each pupil to receive and confess Jesus Christ as Saviour and Lord

As our Lord sought to awaken the faith of the disciples in Himself as the only Redeemer of God's elect, so the Christian teacher must recognize his responsibility for so presenting the Captain of our salvation that each pupil will be led to put his full trust in Him and accept Him as his personal Saviour. To this end the teacher will not fail to make clear the way of salvation as revealed in God's Word, to pray earnestly for each pupil, and to seek by tactful, sympathetic means to bring him to a definite acceptance of Christ. Such decisions must come voluntarily and spontaneously as the culmination of a period of careful preparation, and must be free from artificial or high pressure methods. Acceptance of Christ as Saviour will be only the first step. The Christian teacher will not rest content until he has led each pupil to accept Christ as Lord of his life, into a place of complete surrender and yieldedness to Him.

3. Prepare and train each pupil to fulfill God's purpose in his life

God has a plan for every one of His children. He seldom discloses it in early life, but in His Word we are able to find ample directions as to the preparation that will best fit one for God's program. The young Christian must "grow in grace, and in the knowledge of our Lord and Saviour Jesus Christ." To this end the teacher must be a life-builder as well as a soul-winner. It is his responsibility to heed the divine commission, "Feed my lambs" (John 21:15). Those who have come into newness of life must be fed with the bread of heaven and must be given drink from the fountain of life.

Only as they are so nurtured by instruction in the Scriptures can they develop spiritually. Such development of Christian character results from an increasing knowledge of God's Word and constant obedience to His will as revealed in His Word; from continual acknowledgment of Jesus Christ as Lord of the life, and from daily fellowship with God through prayer.

Spiritual growth should find expression in:

a. Worship

Through worship the Christian enters into the experience of God's reality and nearness, and into a sense of fellowship with Him. Hence an essential part of the teacher's work is the cultivation of the devotional life of the pupils through the class sessions and through the services of the church as a whole. The training should include the cultivation of reverence, gratitude, love, and faith. To this end instruction should be given in the use of songs and stories, and the types of prayers best suited to different classes and departments. Such training requires that the members of the Sunday school be given opportunity to worship. One learns to worship through worshiping. One learns to pray through praying.

Instruction should also be given to help pupils establish daily habits of private prayer and devotional reading. To obtain the desired results, mechanical devices, such as pledges secured and records kept, should always be subordinated to cultivating the spirit of worship and devotion, through this daily observance. It is the spirit rather than the routine of worship that counts and that should be emphasized.

This training in worship as a means of expression of the growing Christian, cannot be given apart from instruction in the Word of God. It bears a vital relation to such instruction and grows out of it. We are instructed as well as inspired to pray. Not only do we have the recorded prayers of eminent

Bible characters, including one of our Lord's, but the Book of Psalms abounds in expressions which without question may be regarded as acceptable forms of devotion.

b. Right living

Someone has said, "The lives our pupils live, measure our success or our failure as teachers." This is true. Unless the truths that have been learned by the pupils find lodgment in their hearts, and then give expression in the daily life and conduct, our teaching is in vain. A person cannot profess to believe one way and act another. Until his faith is consistently manifest by his actions, one is of little value as a witness. Inconsistency must ever be regarded as insincerity. It is the teacher's responsibility to link up the truths taught, with the daily lives of the pupils, in order to help them to be "doers of the word, and not hearers only" (James 1:22), that they may be "living epistles, known and read of all men." If Christians possess the truth as well as profess it, their lives will be transformed. Thus it was in the early Church, when Christians were as ready to die as to dine.

Christian character is dependent upon Christian habits, and Christian habits are dependent upon Christian instruction. We inherit a nature, but we acquire a character by repeated acts. These repeated acts, or habits, are being formed in the lives of every pupil while they are receiving instruction. If your pupils are not forming the good habits of attention, interest, and politeness, they are inevitably, every time you meet them, forming habits of inattention, heedlessness, and rudeness. Schools are habit factories, and a Sunday school where the pupils are noisy, disobedient, discourteous, and irreverent, may be worse for its pupils than no Sunday school at all. Every act of life helps to develop some habit, good or bad. Although the Sunday school teacher has the pupil but once a week, certain impressions can be made and certain habits established that will prove a blessing throughout life. The teacher's opportunity and obligation are to see that everything in the Sunday school tends to the formation of right instead of wrong habits in the pupils.

Childhood is the time for forming good habits. By the age of twelve many habits are established that will remain throughout life. Before the pupil's conversion, the teacher may instruct and train in habits that will help the pupil to become a Christian. Among such habits are regular and punctual attendance at church and Sunday school, Bible study, obedience to parents, reverence for God's day, God's Book, and God's house. These should be in the teacher's thought Sunday morning and during the week, as far as opportunity can be found to follow up the Sunday instruction. After the pupil's conversion, the teacher's aim should be to train in habits that will develop spirituality. It is well if the teacher may have the co-operation of some agency like the Intermediate or Senior Christian Endeavor Society, where the pupils may get still more definite training in habits of public testimony, prayer, reading and quoting Scripture, and discussion of Christian activities.

c. Service

Spiritual growth is also manifest in service, to be rendered not only in the distant future, but now. A growing Christian is an active Christian, ready and eager to serve his Lord. The teacher's privilege and responsibility are to suggest opportunities for a pupil's activity. Such opportunities may be found in the home, school, and church. One of the great benefits of church organization is that it provides work for its members. Once the Sunday school pupil becomes identified with the church, he should be in line for the large number of possible opportunities for service that the organization permits. If there is a well-organized Sunday school, officers will be needed for each department. A large number of members can be utilized as teachers and substitute teachers. Many Sunday schools today are employing from one hundred to two hundred regular workers, besides a variable number for special tasks. These opportunities are multiplied when a church operates branch Sunday schools.

Then in addition, there are the large possibilities for service to be found in the young people's society. This organization can arrange for tract distribution, visitation of the sick, meetings in local missions, hospitals, and jails, and open air services. Every one can do something.

The training in service should not only include the giving of time and strength, but the giving of money, liberally, systematically, and cheerfully, for worthy causes. Indeed, the giving habit needs to be acquired early, and should be a part of the training in worship.

If those who thus serve can say, "The love of Christ constraineth us"; if they heed the admonition, "Whatsoever ye do in word or in deed, do all in the name of the Lord Jesus," their service will be acceptable unto Him whom they serve. They will not only experience growth in grace and joy in service, but will receive hereafter the reward to be bestowed upon the faithful.

QUESTIONS

1. Why is it necessary for the teacher to have a definite aim?
2. Give three reasons why an aim is important.
3. What suggestions are given by White, Carmack and Schmauk?
4. Compare the aims of Christian education suggested by Dr. Reu and Dr. Eavey.
5. What were the three objectives of our Lord's teaching?
6. Quote John 10:10 and Mark 8:36, 37.

7. Upon what was God's offer of the more abundant life dependent?

8. Show how our Lord closely adhered to His objectives.

9. What should be the threefold aim of the Christian teacher?

10. How do we know that God has a gracious and glorious purpose for His child?

11. Why must a teacher be a life-builder as well as a soul-winner?

12. In what three ways must spiritual growth find expression?

13. What is the teacher's responsibility for the formation of right habits?

7

Aids

A N "AID" is all that the word implies. It is not an end in itself, nor is it a crutch upon which the teacher may depend. It is a means of assistance for improving instruction. Good teaching employs the method of showing, not as a device merely to get attention and form a point of contact, but to help pupils form mental pictures, for clearer understanding. These aids should be employed while the pupils read, discuss, are questioned, and are giving expression to their instruction. When a teacher can make use of visual aids while talking, the mind can grasp the story more clearly and remember it more permanently. In other words, eye-gate combines with ear-gate to create the impression.

I. AIDS FOR IMPRESSION

Since it is the primary purpose of the teacher to reach the mentality, there should first be a consideration of such aids as will deepen and render more permanent the impressions.

1. Teacher's manual

At the top of all aids we must put the teacher's manual; not that it is necessarily first in importance, but because it is so largely used. The manual is the teacher's expert helper.[1] It is the guide and counselor of the specialist. The average

[1] J. P. Berkeley, *You Can Teach*, p. 49.

teacher can get a great deal of help from one who is a Bible student and who has obtained a mastery of his textbook through a prescribed course of training. But this expert counselor will also be familiar with the psychological and pedagogical laws covering the teaching of the Bible. The ordinary Sunday school teacher does not have the time to take a training course that would make him, or her, as efficient as a public school teacher. More experienced persons, therefore, put the results of their labors upon the printed page. But no teacher must ever permit the manual to become a crutch, or let it come between him and his pupils. After all, it is essential to remember we are not teaching the contents of manuals. We are teaching pupils. The teaching process requires human relationships. In this connection the teacher's manual can be made an invaluable aid, when the teacher makes it a point to

a. Use it with the Bible

It is most unfortunate when the teacher's manual is used as a substitute for the Bible. If, in preparing the lesson, the teacher will always make it a point to read carefully from his Bible the lesson text and the Scripture relating to it before taking up his quarterly, the task will be approached in the proper order. There is very little real Bible teaching today, because the teachers are satisfied to limit their instruction to the contents of their manual. In a course like the *All-Bible Graded Series,* there is more Bible in the lesson helps than many teachers realize. This provision of additional Bible material is not intended to lengthen the prescribed lesson, but to give the teacher a better background from which to understand and explain the lesson.

b. Use it for the pupil

Attention has been called to the fact that we are teaching the pupil and not the contents of a manual. In other words, we need to be reminded of that fundamental—teaching the

Bible *to* John or Mary. Ministering to the souls of pupils means serving them at the point of their deepest needs, in the life they are actually living. When a manual is consulted with a view to discovering how best to impart the biblical content, in the light of the characteristics and needs of the pupil, it will help the teacher to a more intelligent understanding of his pupils. The teacher's work is conditioned by the pupils' interests, and he succeeds only insofar as he is able rightly to relate the contents of the manual to the pupils' desires and comprehension.

c. Use it out of class

The properly prepared teacher will make little use of a manual during a class period. In fact, it would be better if he would leave it at home, and depend entirely upon his Bible. This will not only constantly remind the pupils of the inspired Source of the teacher's instruction, but will give them a new appreciation of the Bible's contents. While it is important that the manual should never come between the teacher and the pupils, it is even more important that it should not stand between the pupils and the Bible. Then the attention is upon the Bible—the real textbook—and not upon any material compiled even by an experienced writer.

2. Objects

Language is the great tool of the teacher. Human communication is largely through the spoken and written word. Language has its limitations. Words that are not familiar, and sentences that are not comprehensible, are useless. Pupils may fail to grasp a truth through the ear-gate, but they will be far more successful in comprehending what is taught through the eye-gate. Teachers who have made a practice of using visual aids, have no doubt as to their value, but what is needed is a new appreciation of their use, and a wider acquaintance with what aids are available. Teachers who use visual aids have noticed the increased interest of their pupils. They have observed how much more quickly attention can be gained, and the more enthusiastic response that is given. As one has expressed it, "They never look puzzled when you show them pictures."

Objects appeal to all ages. Small objects, linked definitely to the lesson, may be used at any time. A scroll, for instance, will help the pupils to understand how the Old Testament was originally written. Dr. Reu tells of one teacher who brought into his class a homemade model of stocks (Acts 16:24), to picture more vividly and impressively the painful torture of Paul and Silas in prison. Another teacher, while telling the story of Mary anointing our Lord in Bethany (John 12:1–8), took a bottle of perfume and poured some on her handkerchief, then waved it round about until the room was filled with the odor. This story will not be forgotten easily by her pupils. A third teacher, while discussing Hebrews 4:12, showed a double-edged dagger to a class of restless boys. Instantly they became attentive, and certainly received an unforgettable picture of the penetrating power of the Bible.[2]

So we see that a most valuable and effective means of illustration is employed when the teacher, instead of using descriptive words, actually gives the pupil firsthand experience with the thing that is being discussed. A well-equipped Sunday school will be provided with as good a collection as possible of Bible and missionary models and curios.

3. Maps and pictures

Maps are a necessity, especially for pupils who are studying geography in public school, to help them become familiar with the topography, as well as the locations of countries and cities named in the Bible. Maps should be frequently con-

[2] Reu, *How to Teach in the Sunday School*, p. 75.

sulted, and those which can be rolled up when not in use are preferable, as they not only take the smallest amount of space but also last longer. Every teacher should have access to a globe, as it will be valuable not only in locating mission fields, but also in comparing the size and location of Bible lands with the pupils' own country. The use of pictures is so common and time-honored that there is scarcely a teacher, especially of children, who does not employ them. However, it is necessary that the lesson be carefully planned around the pictures, so that the latter do not become the end of the instruction.

The Christian teacher will be on the lookout for good pictures, collecting them from various sources. The life of Christ can be studied by means of a series of masterpieces. Telling the story in combination with using the pictures helps pupils form clearer conceptions. A class which is able by means of a dozen good pictures to give a running narrative of the life of Christ, from His birth to the resurrection, will have the facts more definitely fixed in mind than if limited to one whose instruction has been merely hearing the story. On the other hand, when too much attention is given to a picture, or it contains too many details, it is more likely to be remembered than the lesson.

4. The blackboard

While blackboards are being widely used by departmental superintendents, too few teachers have recognized their advantages. Where there is sufficient blackboard space in a classroom, the board can be used alike by teacher and pupils. The action itself on the part of the teacher in making use of a blackboard helps to sustain attention. Its greater usefulness, however, is to clarify the instruction by means of diagrams and outlines, and even drawings. Care must be taken to avoid details. If the diagram or outline is built up step by step, as the information is imparted, the pupils will enjoy a splendid advantage.

A teacher need not be an artist to use a blackboard effectively. On such a board, a dozen vertical lines will represent the twelve spies going out to investigate the promised land. Ten horizontal lines and two vertical lines will represent the return of these men, with the unfavorable report of the majority. New and difficult words, important dates, can be written down. Also, points can be jotted down in an outline or summary of the instruction.

5. Flannelgraph

No modern teaching aid is so versatile as the flannelgraph, and more and more teachers are employing it. A few Christian workers introduced the use of the flannelgraph visual aids about two decades ago, and it is now widely used in the Sunday school, Daily Vacation Bible school, and in Child Evangelism meetings.

The flannelgraph is a simple device enabling the teacher to build a scene or a diagram before the eyes of the class by merely placing cutout pictures against the surface of the board. The figures adhere to the board because they are backed with flannel. For ordinary use, no special lighting is required, and the equipment may be used indoors or out-of-doors. The materials and equipment are easily transported from place to place in a relatively small, compact parcel. The cost can be kept at a minimum because the equipment can be improvised, or made even by an amateur. More elaborate equipment and exquisitely designed materials are available at reasonable, higher cost. The use of the flannelgraph is not confined to this country. Missionaries in far-off fields of the world, enthusiastically welcome this aid in their unique teaching problems. The problem of communicating is quickly solved through this medium of reaching the eye-gate.

The flannelgraph secures the attention at the very outset, and if the story is kept moving and new factors appear often, it effectively sustains the interest. If the class is taught to repeat the story at the end of the lesson, the pupils in placing the figures upon the board will combine not only the faculties of hearing and seeing, but also of seeing and doing.

Frank G. Coleman, in *The Romance of Winning Children*, says there are three fundamentals the teacher must master if the flannelgraph is to serve its full purpose:

a. The principle of dexterity

Unskillful fumbling as you manipulate the figures of your flannelgraph lesson is distracting. It calls attention away from your lesson to your own lack of skill. The teacher should practice. The teacher should not only know his story well but also practice telling it with the use of the flannelgraph figures, until he is thoroughly familiar with it. Then everything should be in readiness for your class session, and the figures arranged on an adjoining table, in the order in which they are to be used, so that the hands can be kept as free as possible. Keep the story moving. Talk while you work, and do not turn away entirely from the class while using the board.

b. Suspense

Curiosity, which we have already noted is an important factor in gaining attention, is aroused by the way the figures are placed on the board. If the back is held up before the class, they will be curious to know what is on the other side. Nor is this curiosity satisfied until the last word has been spoken, and the teacher is ready to place it on the board. Never place any of the materials on the board before you begin to speak. Develop the scene as you tell the story; and then delay that development to the last possible moment.

c. *Movement*

Attention has already been called to the fact that the use of the blackboard brings the teacher into action. If he walks about, as he tells the story with the flannelgraph, his movement will be equally helpful in sustaining attention. Every motion or gesture occupies the eye, and even though many may be seemingly unnecessary, they will put life into the instruction.[3]

6. Projector

The projector is also a modern aid. While David Livingstone, in his African journeys, used a magic lantern to gain the interest and friendship of the natives, the modern projector is being used advantageously for the same purpose in enlightened countries. The stereopticon, which the American lecturer once used to illustrate his address, had a slide of glass which measured $3\frac{1}{4}$ inches by 4 inches. In Britain the glass slides were square. But in recent years, a new type of miniature slide, available in film transparencies and measuring two inches by two inches, is commonly used.

The popularity of these miniature slides is due to several factors. The projector required is more easily carried and less expensive. The slides are not easily broken and their weight is but a fraction of that of the old glass transparencies. The development of the 35 mm. high-speed miniature camera has made it possible to produce homemade slides at a small expense. Perhaps the most important contribution to the teacher's work has been the Kodachrome film which has made it possible to reproduce scenes and pictures in full color on slides, at a fraction of the cost of hand-coloring the old glass transparencies.

In recent years educators have made careful experiments

[3] Frank G. Coleman, *The Romance of Winning Children*, p. 146.

in the use of the projector as an advance means of instruction. The results from these experiments have disappointed some of the early enthusiasts who supposed that much of our instruction would be done from the screen. On the other hand, they have constantly shown that teaching with the use of projectors is superior to teaching without them.

For the Sunday school teacher, it is doubtful that a projector can ever be regarded as more than a supplementary means of instruction. Much information must accompany the picture to make it practical and helpful. Perhaps the best use, especially of the moving picture, will be reviews of a series of lessons.

II. AIDS FOR EXPRESSION

A real distinction needs to be made between aids for impression and aids for expression. We have but to recall the need for the teacher's reaching the personality in order to understand the place of aids for expression.

1. Importance

Visual aids, after all, are helps for reaching the mentality. But even if the pupil is better informed and is able to retain his information, the visual aids have not necessarily secured a response. Expression aids are important for

a. Deepening the impression

Someone has said, "A little child will probably forget what he hears; he may forget what he has seen; he will not forget what he has done." If this is true, it follows that we must think of learning not as a process limited to listening and looking, but also of doing. Aids for expression furnish opportunity for doing on the part of the pupils. As the pupil expresses these ideas, he reimpresses them upon his own mind, and he gets them now through a different sense channel—not only through eye and ear, but also through the hand.

Whatever may be the kind of learning, there is one law which stands out as the first law of learning anything—pupils *learn by doing.* Learning begins and continues in what the learner does. The pupil taking a piano lesson may get certain impressions from what he hears and sees when the teacher demonstrates a musical selection, but he doesn't really begin to learn until he practices the piece himself. Until practice begins there can be no real learning.

b. Capitalizing on energy

Pupils like to do things. It has been known that among the best solutions for problems of discipline is keeping the active pupil occupied. He has boundless energy which needs to be utilized. It is far better for the teacher to use this natural disposition to activity rather than to have to work against it. Nothing is more typical of childhood, or more trying sometimes, than the boundless energy and ceaseless activity of boys and girls. The wise teacher uses this activity and energy, directs it, controls it, instead of trying to suppress it. Rightly directed expressional activity can serve an excellent educational purpose. Attempts to suppress it may bring disastrous results.

c. Reaching the personality

In a former chapter we have seen that we have not successfully contacted the personality until there has been the appropriation and application of knowledge. This is not in the realm of the teacher's instruction, but in the response that is obtained from the pupil. The teacher himself is probably the best visual aid that can ever be placed before a pupil. His class constantly sees before them the life ideal to which they may attain. An unconscious imitation of a noble character may be the appropriation of something more valuable even than the instruction imparted. In reaching the personality through expressional aids, we are doing far more than providing "busy" work for restless pupils. The activities are to have a positive value in shaping a life. Our aim is the development of Christian character and training in Christian living.

2. Pupil's manual

Far more important than any visual aid for impression is the pupil's manual. Next to the teacher's quarterly is this work-book for the pupil. It represents his best response to the instruction. Of course the pupil's manual is a means and not an end. If the teacher is more concerned that his class should be able to show a neat and orderly manual than that they should have the training that comes from doing the work in this manual, he is defeating the ultimate purpose of the activity. No lesson series is complete without these pupil's manuals. In fact, they are even more important than the teacher's manual, and a good lesson writer will generally prepare the pupil's manual first.

It is preferable that the work in the pupil's manual be done at home, for then the teacher has a foundation of knowledge to which he can contribute additional instruction. The chief mistake made by teachers is the lack of attention given to these all-important manuals. Often the books are carelessly given out, with a formal suggestion or request that they be studied at home, in preparation of the lesson for the following Sunday. But unless there is co-operation in the home, the chances are there will be no preparation, and the books will be forgotten or lost. Under these circumstances, it is best to use at least a part of the class period for supervised study. If there is any written work provided in the book it can be cared for at this time. Many good teachers follow this method of using the pupil's manual, and get splendid results. Above all, they have learned the pedagogical principle that teaching is getting a response, and that it is more important for the pupil to prepare the notebook than for the teacher to spend the class period in talking.

In every pupil's manual there should be

a. *Something to write*

There may be blanks to fill in, sentences to complete. The act of writing is not only the pupil's recording of knowledge, but can also be a personal response to that instruction.

b. *Something to find*

When a pupil is required to search the archives of knowledge for an answer, he is more likely to remember the results of his work, and his activity will also make an impression upon his personality, developing his initiative for the discovery of truth.

c. *Something to draw*

The pupil may see a map, and so be helped to a better understanding of the lesson, but he will gain his best impression by drawing it. Blackboard work is equal in value to filling blank pages in a pupil's manual. In drawing a map, it is not necessary that an artistic sketch be provided. The right hand boundary for a map of Palestine is the Sea of Galilee and the Dead Sea, with the Jordan River connecting. With this are a half dozen important cities—names to be printed in large distinct letters. When the pupils have learned to locate on their maps, Palestine, Capernaum, Nazareth, Jericho, Bethlehem, and Bethany (located north to south in a straight line) they have the geographical essentials for the life of Christ. To this knowledge other items can readily be added.

3. Constructions

Marion Lawrance first called the attention of Sunday school teachers to the fact that a child remembers 10 per cent of what he hears, 50 per cent of what he sees, 70 per cent of what he says, and 90 per cent of what he does. What he writes and finds and draws will make a more indelible impression upon his mind than what he sees, but in all probability he will best remember what he constructs. It was the advent of the Daily Vacation Bible school that first attracted the attention of educators to the importance of manual arts in religious instruction. The Sunday school hour was too brief for the time required. A few teachers were familiar with the success of this means of instruction in the public schools. Only a few Bible institutes were offering courses in manual arts. Moreover, there was a prejudice against having the pupil waste his time in this field. At best, many religious leaders thought that manual expression served no higher purpose that providing "busy" work. The success of manual arts in the public school led to its adoption in the Daily Vacation Bible school. It was seen that pupils were not wasting time when their constructions were closely correlated to instruction. Handwork served a very practical purpose. The fact was soon discovered that in their love for doing things, pupils were more anxious to attend the three hours of vacation school than the one hour of Sunday school. Further, the Scripture Press found it necessary, in connection with their own Vacation Bible school lessons, to supply some pre-session activities for boys and girls who insisted on coming to school before the opening hour. Even a three-hour session was none too long for their period of learning.

a. Materials

There are many inexpensive materials available for construction purposes. Paper and pasteboard lend themselves to the making of many projects. The Bible village, or a house representing each book, can be constructed entirely of paper. The girls can work with cloth, and the boys with wood, to good advantage. These materials are inexpensive and call for a small outlay of money.

b. Projects

A boy will learn more about the Tabernacle from constructing a model, than by reading the directions in Exodus a hundred times. The construction of a relief map of Palestine will give him a better conception of the mountains and valleys than any amount of reading about them, or even special instruction in Bible geography. A resourceful teacher will discover innumerable projects that can be related to a Bible lesson. One has only to scan the pages of the pupil's manual of the *All Bible Vacation School Series* to gain an impression of the possibilities for providing these activities for the pupils.

Finally, aids for expression must go further than the development of the personality. This is important. But for the Christian teacher there is a higher objective. He must reach the spiritual life of his pupils. Without discounting in the least the value of activity in the classroom as a means of making impressions more vivid, more permanent, and more vital, and appealing to the personality for choice and decision, the Christian teacher must aim for the development of Christian character and training in Christian living. Character and ability to live the Christian life will come only through practice— practice in Christian living. For this reason, in a subsequent chapter, considerable attention will be given to making application of instruction to the spiritual life of the pupil.

QUESTIONS

1. What is meant by an aid?
2. Name five aids for the impression of truth.
3. What is the teacher's manual, and in what three ways should it be used?
4. Why are objects helpful in teaching?
5. Discuss the value of maps and pictures.

6. What use can be made of the blackboard?

7. What are Mr. Coleman's three fundamentals for the use of the flannelgraph?

8. Why is the projector only a supplementary means of instruction?

9. Give three reasons why aids for expression are important.

10. Why is the pupil's manual of such great importance?

11. How can the pupil's manual be used for supervised study?

12. What three lines of activity should be subscribed in the pupil's manual?

13. Discuss briefly the value of manual arts.

14. Suggest several biblical projects that lend themselves to constructive activity.

Part III: *The Pupil*

8

Point of Contact

I F THE teacher is to share the learning process with the pupil, the point of contact between the two is of the greatest importance. Every teaching activity must have some sort of beginning. We must start somewhere. This starting point is in some respects the most important part of the procedure. Success or failure may largely depend upon the approach. If attention and interest are not secured then, it is useless to proceed. We need to be reminded of the old proverb, "Well begun is half done."

Apparent inattention, however, does not necessarily mean a total lack of attention. The boy with the far-away look in his eyes is paying attention—but not to you. One cannot teach either without or against the attention. Such effort is like pulling a car without its motor running, or pulling it with the gear in reverse. Until the teacher has secured the attention of the class, there is no need to go on. "The difference between a trained teacher and a novice," said Edward Leigh Pell, "is never more apparent than in the first five minutes of the lesson hour. The novice looks first at the lesson. The trained teacher looks first at the pupils."

Without attention there can be no learning. Most so-called teaching is merely so much talk. The pupil hears you, but he does not attend to what you are saying. It is not teaching unless the pupil gives attention to the truths you teach. He must not only be conscious of them, but he must focus attention on them and think of them. Unless he carefully lays away the truths in his mental storehouse, there is no learning.

It is not the pupil's fault if a teacher is not commanding his attention. The janitor of Henry Ward Beecher's church asked if he should awaken any members of the congregation who might fall asleep during the sermon. "No," the great preacher replied, "come to the pulpit and wake me up." [1] The teacher must assume responsibility for inattention.

We all like to see a group of soldiers at drill. Their actions are simultaneous and uniform. When a commander says, "Attention!" all heads and eyes are turned to the front. From that moment every movement is made with promptness and precision. A teacher can get the same attention from his class. It is well to observe how marvelously the Lord Jesus Christ succeeded in making the point of contact. Whether He was dealing with His friends or His enemies, He connected up with their minds. A striking example is His discussion with the woman at Jacob's well. The teaching situation was difficult. Almost every conceivable obstacle stood in the way. The woman had come for water, not to receive instruction. They were poles apart in the groups they represented. Christ was a Jew, and the woman, a Samaritan—and the two peoples had no dealings with each other. Yet our Lord broke through all these barriers with the simplest, most natural introduction that could be made—a request for a drink of water.

Whatever method the teacher may employ, his first task is to get a point of contact. There are two contacts to be made at the very beginning of the instruction. The first is,

[1] Frank G. Coleman, *The Romance of Winning Children*, p. 54.

I. CONTACT WITH THE PUPIL

1. Defining attention

Attention is concentrated consciousness. Inattention is attention to something different from what is being presented. Briefly, inattention is attention to the wrong thing. When we do not have the attention of our pupils, someone or something else does have it. The teacher has competition. Perhaps this competition arises from external distractions—outside sights and sounds, interruptions by officers and visitors, or uncomfortable seats, and rooms that have extreme temperatures. Separate classrooms and comfortable and appropriate furniture assist in securing attention.

But the distractions are not all external. The pupil may sit in the class, and to all outward appearances be absorbed in what is going on, and yet be a thousand miles away in thought, as far as getting something out of the lesson. He is mentally absent. The teacher must compete with many absorbing things that so easily crowd out of the pupil's mind the things we should like to have there.

a. Types

There are several classes of attention, each of which has a variety of degrees of intensity.

(1). Involuntary

This attention is of the flitting kind, and is obedient to any distractions that may arise. A loud noise, a bright light, a strong contrast of any kind, will occasion involuntary attention. Someone may rap on the door, or enter the room, and attention is diverted. Something conspicuous in the teacher's dress or manner will turn the attention from the instruction to the instructor.

(2). Voluntary

Attention may be compelled by disciplinary measures, or

an appeal to the power of the will of the pupil. We are trying to study and we find our minds wandering. By an act of will we bring ourselves back to our work. We try to distinguish a person's words from the noise of a machine. We seek to pick out the mistakes of punctuation without reference to spelling or style or content.

H. Clay Trumbull tells of a young man who applied to a dry goods jobber for a position as salesman. "Can you sell the goods?" was the merchant's first question. "I can sell the goods to any man who really wants to buy," was the qualified rejoinder. "Oh, nonsense!" said the merchant, "Anybody can sell goods to a man who really wants to buy. I want salesmen who can sell goods to men who don't want to buy." [2]

It is comparatively easy to teach those who really want to be taught; to hold the attention of those who are determined to be attentive, but there is a real problem in getting and holding the attention of students whose thoughts are flying in every direction save that of the lesson of the day. For the teacher to attempt to force attention is futile. Banging a ruler on the table, or slamming a book down hard, or vigorously ringing a bell, or clapping hands, will summon a pupil from his far-away thoughts. The teacher may elevate his voice, and exhort the pupil, "Pay attention now!" "Look right at me!" "Listen to me!" This forced attention is only temporary. The more a teacher resorts to pounding on a table or raising his voice, the less effective these means become.

(3). *Nonvoluntary*

Pupils learn most readily when they are so "absorbed" in their study as to be oblivious to what is going on around them. A visitor called one day on the musician, Edvard Grieg. Mrs. Grieg duly notified him to come downstairs. He replied, "Yes." As he did not come down, he was reminded several times that

[2] Trumbull, *Teaching and Teachers*, p. 139.

a man was in the parlor waiting to see him. Twelve o'clock came and went. At three o'clock it was found necessary to go up and forcibly persuade him to take something to eat. He was so absorbed in a new composition that he scarcely noticed even this interruption. It is this kind of attention that has brought about most of the world's progress in the arts and sciences.

b. Scope

The range of attention is limited to a very small field— seldom more than six objects at a time, usually not more than one. The intensity of the attention is lessened as the scope is increased. This experiment can be tried in any class. Put five words on the board. Let them remain there for five seconds before erasing them. Then let every member of the class write into his notebook all he can remember. Next, write ten words and let them remain for five seconds before erasing. Again have the class reproduce what can be remembered. Finally, permit the class to see twenty-five words for five seconds and then record their impressions. It will be found that while nearly all of them remember the five words, less than half of them can reproduce the ten words, and less than one-fifth of them the twenty-five words.

c. Duration

The attention fluctuates. No matter how fascinating the story, or how interesting the conversation, it is impossible for anyone to keep the attention on it all the time. The longest stretch of attention recorded in a psychological laboratory is said to be twenty-four seconds. The average is about five or six seconds.

2. Gaining attention

The average boy, as he comes to class, is not thinking of what will be taught. His mind is elsewhere. Indeed, he may be so intent on some other thing which monopolizes his attention that the lesson may be approached with protest, if not with prejudice. How then may a right attitude on the part of the pupil be secured?

a. Vary the approach

A class should never be greeted, or a lesson commenced, twice in exactly the same way. Variety of method of approach is bound to gain attention. Sometimes the teacher will apply to the eye-gate. At other times something unusual will be said. It is only when we habitually follow the same formula of expression that we fail at the outset to gain attention.

A certain minister, one Sunday morning, instead of announcing his text as usual, leaned over his pulpit and said, "My friends, I am going to ask you a plain question; but it is a question that not one of you can answer. In fact, it is a question that I can't answer myself. If an angel from heaven came down here now and I should ask him this question, he couldn't answer it." By that time the preacher had the attention of the entire congregation. Then came the question, which was thus made a sermon in itself: "What shall it profit a man, if he shall gain the whole world, and lose his own soul?" [3] Variety in approach secures immediate attention.

The interest in a large class of men was explained by one of the members, "The teacher always keeps us guessing. We never know what he is going to do. He never does the same thing twice in the same way. Every Sunday we know that we are going to get something good, but we do not know what it is." This teacher understood human nature very well, and he was willing to make such preparation that he could maintain the interest of his class from week to week.

b. Arouse curiosity

Many expert teachers realize the value, pedagogically, of the trait which we call curiosity. This characteristic is espe-

[3] Trumbull, *op. cit.,* p. 142.

cially marked in younger children, but older people have also been known to be curious. This propensity to discover things is used to advantage by the teacher who plans some surprise to be introduced in his lesson. Dr. A. H. McKinney tells of one primary teacher who always had an object picture, or something else, with which to surprise her pupils. However, it was always kept concealed until the psychological time for its release.[4] "Teacher, what have you in your bag today?" was a question with which she was frequently greeted. To this she had a ready answer, which tended to whet the curiosity of the questioner, who soon spread the news through the room— "Teacher has something fine to show us today." On the Sunday when she wished to impress the fact that evil companions lead those associated with them into evil, she had a fine red apple in her bag. For some time the children had no idea of what was coming. At the proper moment, the teacher produced the apple and began to talk about it, dwelling particularly on its form and beauty. Her pupils were all alive with interest when she turned to a spot that had been covered and showed them that it was bruised. It took but a little effort to get the children to imagine how the effects of that bruise would spread, and the beautiful apple soon become a mass of decay. But the gist of what she wished to teach was understood, for this skilled instructor had made use of the God-given trait of curiosity in such a way that she had led on step by step until her little ones fully comprehended the point she endeavored to make.

At one time, Dr. John H. Vincent (originator, with Lewis Miller, of Chautauqua Movement) in talking to a group of teachers, took a piece of chalk between his thumb and finger and turned with it toward the blackboard on the platform in the sight of his class. "Just look here!" he said, holding the

[4] McKinney, *Practical Pedagogy in the Sunday School,* p. 62.

chalk near the board. Every eye in the room was intent upon him. "That is all!" he said, as he dropped his hand at his side and turned back to the class. "I only wanted your attention." [5]

Hold up a curio before your class, and hear the inevitable question, "What is that?" Attention will follow curiosity as surely as the day follows night. Sometimes merely the expression, "Once upon a time," and the children are in readiness for a story. Sometimes a well-directed question will awaken curiosity. Ask your class, "What is the fifteenth book in the Old Testament?" and watch them begin to count. [6]

c. Appeal to the individual

Jesus knew how to gain the attention of His hearers. With great skill He won the curious publican, Zaccheus, who had climbed up a sycamore tree that he might see the Master as He passed that way. Jesus looked up and saw Zaccheus—establishing a point of contact with his look of sincerity and interest. This point was strengthened when the Master directly addressed Zaccheus, and then was made permanent by His saying, "Make haste and come down, for today I must abide in thy house."

3. Sustaining attention

It is one thing to gain attention, and quite another to sustain it. Sometimes it is well to have

a. Change of procedure

How is it possible for boys and girls to get so much enjoyment out of a session of the Daily Vacation Bible school, which lasts so much longer than the Sunday school hour? The frequent change that we find in the program is what makes it so interesting. For the most part, these programs are much more carefully prepared and executed, and lack the monotony of the Sunday school period. Perhaps one of the best contri-

[5] Trumbull, *op. cit.,* p. 144.
[6] Coleman, *op. cit.,* p. 99.

butions the Daily Vacation Bible school has made to the church is that it has provided some splendid suggestions for gaining and sustaining the attention of boys and girls.

The story is told of Spurgeon, the peerless preacher, that on one occasion when he was preaching, on a warm Sunday afternoon, he noticed that some of his hearers were nodding. He stopped his discourse and cried, "Fire, fire, fire!" Immediately his audience was all attention, and those who had been slumbering looked around as if to inquire, "Where is the fire?" Anticipating this question, the preacher said, "The fire is in hell for such sleepy sinners as you are."

Experienced teachers use different means for wooing wandering attention. They walk rapidly across the platform, or make quick gestures, or otherwise suddenly introduce new motion. Sometimes merely a prolonged pause will awaken the wanderer to inquire why the monotony of instruction has ceased.

Jesus knew how to hold as well as awaken the attention of His hearers. The impression one obtains on reading the Gospels is that He had even better attention at the close of His discourses than at the beginning. The same means that Jesus used to win attention was also used to hold attention. He used great variety of form and imagery in His messages, and changed from one subject to another as the occasion demanded. In the Sermon on the Mount, the picture changes with nearly every verse.

b. Arousing interest

Nonvoluntary attention is based on interest. Artificial means may be employed for gaining and holding attention, but the attention that can be produced by the least effort is based upon interest. The reason that baseball and football and fishing and dolls are so absorbing to boys and girls is that they appeal to something vital in their nature. They satisfy a need, which cannot be denied or disregarded. The Sunday school teacher may attempt to compete with them and fail, but if he can make games work for him instead of against him he will succeed. In brief, the only way to get and hold the attention of boys and girls is by making the work of the Sunday school class of vital interest to them. An interested class is an attentive class. How then can we get our classes interested?

To answer this question, we must go back to our study of the personality. We remember that it is one thing for the teacher to reach the intellect, and quite another to reach the personality. While the provision of knowledge would be an intellectual attainment, only the creation of interest would affect the personality. Here the personality of the teacher becomes an important factor, and the teacher-pupil relationship the supreme means of arousing and sustaining interest. If Jesus showed great skill in awakening and holding the attention and interest of His disciples, it was in no small measure due to the fact that He knew how to establish a point of contact with His hearers. Whether He was speaking with His friends, or addressing His enemies, He knew the place where their minds as well as their interests were.

Note how successful Jesus was in awakening interest in the minds and hearts of His disciples. Very early in His ministry, Peter, James and John, and other disciples, forsook all and followed Him. Wherever our Lord went, He was accompanied by the disciples. Even when the prospect of success was becoming dim, Thomas exclaimed, "Let us also go, that we may die with him" (John 11:16). At another time, Peter declared, in the face of the most discouraging circumstances, that though all men should forsake the Lord, yet he would remain loyal. The interest of the disciples was so great that, with one exception, they all remained loyal to the last.

II. APPERCEPTION

Two of the most important principles of pedagogy have to do with interest and apperception. Interest, which we have found to be such an important element in gaining and sustaining attention, looks forward. Apperception, which we are now about to consider, looks backward. The student's desire to learn is interest. When he connects new knowledge with what he already possesses we have apperception.

We have stated that attention is secured by appealing to the pupil's interest. Now the teacher has the responsibility of showing why he has sought that interest. The teacher knows the truth he desires the pupil to know, but the pupil does not know it yet. It is, therefore, necessary for the teacher to make clear to the pupil what he is attempting to teach. It is not now a question for the teacher, whether the truth he would teach is the most important truth in the world. It is enough that it is the truth he is now trying to teach. But this new truth cannot be grasped by the pupil except in the light of his past experiences. This process then of acquiring new ideas by the aid of knowledge already acquired, is called apperception.

There should exist a perfect harmony between interest and apperception. The learner is not simply interested, but he is interested in *something*. That something is a part of the pupil's little world which he has picked out from the great world about him. "It is the object of parents and teachers," says Professor O. M. Norlie, "to enrich his world of experience and interest." [7] The law of interest has a twofold value. We become interested in the things to which we give attention, and we give attention to the things in which we are interested.

Apperception, we have already noted, looks backward. We

[7] Norlie, *An Elementary Christian Psychology*, p. 200.

interpret the present in the light of our past experiences. This is not only one of the basic laws of pedagogy, but its practice makes learning easier and quicker. Not that there is any easy road to learning, but there is a natural process which greatly accelerates the progress of acquisition, just as it is better to follow a highway than to stumble along through brush or over broken ground. Through apperception we use knowledge already acquired as a sort of bridge to new realms of information. The old knowledge explains the new, and it in turn is often enriched and illuminated by it. The new lesson must make a

1. Contact with familiar scenes

Have you ever traveled along a new road? Perhaps you have then observed a great many objects that are familiar scenes along most roads, but now your attention is arrested. That farmhouse looks familiar. You have either been along that road before, or that house is very similar to one you have seen before. Now you are all attention, looking for other objects you might recognize. The attraction of the familiar has taken hold of your attention.

The mind has a tendency to welcome the familiar and to shrink from what it cannot recognize. A new idea presented to the mind is like a person entering a room full of people. If he is an entire stranger, he and everyone else present feels a sense of embarrassment, and he is ill at ease. However, if he discovers one person in the room with whom he is acquainted, he feels much more at home. Likewise when a new idea comes into the mind, if it can find some close relationship with other ideas in the mind, then the new idea feels at home. But if the new idea has no connection with the knowledge already acquired, there is a feeling of strangeness, and it is either treated with indifference or rejected entirely. The first step in the teaching process, then, is to prepare the mind of the pupil by bringing into his consciousness ideas which are related to those contained in the lesson. In so doing, the first advance is made upon the memory. Of course, if the pupil has been studying the lesson before coming to class, he already has some ideas concerning it, and others are easily added. But suppose, as is often the case, he has not studied the lesson. In planning her approach the teacher must fall back upon her knowledge of the pupil and what he is likely to be thinking about. This knowledge she acquires by studying the pupil's home life, his school life, his recreations, his companionships, and his reading. The more the teacher knows about these, the easier it will be to find the point of contact with the pupil's present knowledge.

2. Contrast by association

Apperception includes, in large degree, the matter of contrast—contrasting the new with the old. If the teacher wishes to explain the destruction wrought by the Deluge, he may begin by reminding his class of some flood that has taken place near their home. If he wishes to impress upon their minds how fast sin grew on earth, he may recall some epidemic that spread sickness and death throughout the community. To give pupils some conception of the Temple, he may begin by comparing it with their church building. These old and familiar concepts pave the way and form the foundation for receiving, understanding, and assimilating the new. If we neglect to do this, the new concepts will remain altogether strange and foreign to the class. The children may be able to repeat what the teacher has told, but they will not understand it nor make it their own. Without observing the law of apperception, we can reach neither the personality nor the mentality.

Our Lord made frequent use in His teaching of this law of contrasts. The parable of the sower is based upon familiar scenes in the minds of His audience. It has been suggested that when Jesus spoke this parable on the shore of the Lake of Galilee, He could direct the eyes of His audience to a farmer sowing grain on the hillside. His reference to the wind, in His talk with Nicodemus, to the bread after the feeding of the five thousand, to the lost sheep, the lost coin, and the prodigal son, were all rooted in familiar scenes and experiences in the minds of the people whom He taught.

The address of Paul in the synagogue of Antioch is another good example of the use of this law. Paul did not begin his address by telling about Jesus. The Jews in his audience were deeply prejudiced on that subject, and the Gentiles had probably never heard of the Messiah. So Paul begins by recalling to the minds of the Jews, some of the facts of their national history, as far down as the time of David. Here he found a point of contact, in the promise of God to David, and declared to his attentive audience, "Of this man's seed hath God . . . raised unto Israel a Saviour, Jesus." Then he tells the story of the crucifixion and the resurrection, and proclaims the remission of sins through Christ's name (Acts 13:16–41).

3. Attract through participation

Boys and girls love to do things. By appealing to this interest, a splendid contact can be made for the presentation of unfamiliar truth. Frank G. Coleman tells of an occasion when he brought an entire department in the Sunday school into active participation in his teaching on the Tabernacle. He had the group go outdoors, measure actual distances, and then form a living outline of the Tabernacle and its chief features.[8]

Certainly the child learning to dress himself would never have mastered the lesson had he simply sat and listened. He learned through doing—the way in which nearly all out-of-

[8] Coleman, *op. cit.*, p. 102.

school learning naturally occurs. "Is it not strange," says Professor Gaines S. Dobbins, "that in the classroom we should have overlooked so often this basic principle and depended instead on learning by listening?" [9]

If we study the Gospels, we shall be impressed with the frequency with which Jesus encouraged participation on the part of His disciples. The pedagogical school of the Lord Jesus Christ is most clearly exhibited in the many instances where He caused His disciples to participate in their own instruction. The learning process became a mutual sharing of interest. There was activity with interest and interest with activity. He did only that which the disciples were unable to do. At the beginning of His ministry, He entrusted to His disciples the work of baptizing converts to His cause (John 4:2). He sent forth the twelve disciples to go into all the cities of the land, to proclaim the message of repentance and the imminent coming of the kingdom (Matt. 10:5–7). Our Lord gave to the twelve, and then to the seventy, suggestions as to how their problems might be solved, but left the details in their own hands to work out as best they could.

QUESTIONS

1. How does a trained teacher differ from a novice in making a point of contact?
2. How did our Lord make a point of contact with the woman at Jacob's well?
3. What is meant by attention?
4. Name three types of attention.
5. What is meant by nonvoluntary attention?
6. What is meant by the scope and duration of attention? How can it be tested?
7. Give three suggestions for gaining attention.

[9] Dobbins, *The Improvement of Teaching in the Sunday School,* p. 138.

8. How can curiosity be aroused to secure attention?
9. In what two ways can attention be sustained?
10. Why is interest the key to nonvoluntary attention?
11. Distinguish between interest and apperception.
12. In what three ways can we observe the law of apperception?
13. Show how our Lord and Paul made use of the law of apperception.
14. How did our Lord encourage participation on the part of His disciples?

9

Interrogation

THE REAL test of a teacher is the *response* of his pupils. He must not only instruct, but educate—lead out his pupils. The word "teaching" comes from the Anglo-Saxon derivative *taecho,* meaning, "to show how to do." Teaching, then, is not telling; in fact, often he teaches best who talks least. Teaching of necessity is a probing process in which the surgical instrument is the question. The response of the pupil, like the recovery of the patient, will depend on the skill with which the instrument is used.

Questioning has an important part in the teacher-pupil relationship. It keeps the pupils at work with their teacher to a common end. It accomplishes much in gaining and sustaining attention. It clarifies the truth which is to be taught. But more than anything else, questioning has a large place in making the teacher and the pupils co-workers in the completion of the teaching process.

Anybody can ask questions. But not everybody can ask questions that really teach. There is doubtful value in asking questions from a quarterly and having the pupils respond with the printed answers in front of them. Such a method of questioning cannot do other than deaden the pupils' interest in the Bible and create in them an aversion to the lesson hour. The question is a teaching device or weapon that can be used most powerfully and effectively in skillful hands. Questioning is an art—one of the fine arts—which when once acquired, will be the making of a teacher. Dr. Herman Harrell Horne says, "The interrogation point is the badge of the teaching profession," while Francis Bacon declared that "the skillful question is the half of knowledge."

Our Lord was a master of the art of questioning. In the comparatively brief record of His ministry, more than one hundred questions are recorded. Even the most casual reader of the Gospels cannot help but be impressed with such a large number of startling, unusual, and unexpected questions as He used in His utterances. At the age of twelve He was asking questions, and one of the first utterances of His public ministry was a question addressed to His first two disciples, "What seek ye?" And this earliest of His interrogations is typical of the thought-provoking and reflecting character of all His questions. Even in His declarative discourses He frequently interspersed His statements with such rhetorical questions as, "What think ye?" and "How think ye?" A study of our Lord's questions is a pedagogical course in itself.

I. PURPOSE OF QUESTIONS

To appreciate the value of a good question properly addressed, it is well to know something about its purpose. In the law of the teaching process it was observed that the question was the most important stimulus to the mind, and that the actual educational process begins when a pupil asks questions. It will be seen further that the question is used:

1. To awaken thought

The first object of the teacher in taking up the lesson is to make a point of contact with the pupils in order to arouse interest. Generally this can best be done by a question suited to the mind of the pupils. This question will be like a fisherman's bait on a hook. If it does not appeal to the particular fish he is seeking to catch, the fish will not be attracted. The real problem of the teacher then is to ask such a question as will catch the interest of the pupils and elicit a spontaneous response.

2. To direct thought

Once the mind has been awakened, each succeeding question must grow out of the preceding one and its answer, and all put together must lead in a definite direction toward the goal which the teacher has set. When all such questions have unity and purpose, the minds of the pupils can be successfully carried from one point to another.

3. To quicken thought

The pupil who has a tendency to let his thoughts wander can be recalled by a question. It will throw a burning spark into his mind. An atmosphere of dullness, in which thinking becomes sluggish, can be dissipated by a series of rapid questions. There must be sufficient evidence of life and vivacity to assure a satisfactory rate of progress. Things must move on with a certain rapidity. Questions should be asked quickly and answered just as speedily. If they cannot be answered by one, they should be passed rapidly to another. A barrage of questions will put new life into a stagnant atmosphere.

4. To apply thought

Pupils may be brought to think on a subject without associating it in any way with themselves. The problem is to get them to apply the truth to their own lives. This can frequently be done by a question. Christ was interested in things only as they were related to the lives of men and women. "Whom do men say that I the Son of man am?" He asked His disciples. And when they responded, He quickly applied their thought by the personal question, "But whom say *ye* that I am?"

II. PREPARATION OF QUESTIONS

The use of printed questions read from a quarterly is too mechanical to awaken interest. Such a procedure stifles rather than stimulates. The all-important personality of the teacher is hidden behind a lesson help someone else has created. On the other hand, until an instructor has had experience in the art of oral examination he cannot hope to frame his questions advantageously after coming to class. Almost all extemporaneous preachers write out their outlines. A good teacher will find it worth while to prepare a carefully worded set of questions in advance. Part of the average unwillingness on the part of the pupil to participate in the lesson is due to the teacher's lack of skill in the use of questions. The value of original, written questions will soon be appreciated. In the preparation of such a list there will be need for several types of approach to the pupils' minds.

1. Contact questions

We have already seen that the interrogation is of value in awakening thought. Attention can be gained and interest aroused when the teacher begins the lesson, if an appropriate question has been thought out for the introduction. Many times our Lord used a question for this purpose. Perhaps the most familiar and frequent expression was, "What think ye?" Conversations were also introduced by such inquiries as, "Will ye also go away?" "Unto what is the kingdom of God like?" "Whence shall we buy bread that these may eat?"

2. Rhetorical questions

We have often heard preachers and even teachers asking questions without giving anyone time to answer. Such inquiries are injected into a discourse for effect rather than reply. If they occasion surprise, or issue a challenge, they stimulate mental activity. It is interesting to note how many of these rhetorical questions are to be found in the Sermon on the Mount. "Which of you by taking thought can add one cubit unto his stature?" (Matt. 6:27). "Why take ye thought for raiment?" (Matt. 6:28). "Why beholdest thou the mote that is in thy brother's eye?" (Matt. 7:3). "Do men gather grapes of thorns, or figs of thistles?" (Matt. 7:16). Such questions, even in discourse, throw the responsibility of thinking inescapably on the pupils.

3. Factual questions

Perhaps the easiest questions to answer are those that call for information previously given the pupil. Their greatest value is that the replies fix in the mind the instruction that has already been imparted. Since the work of a teacher is not complete until it has been tested, factual questions will reveal just how much instruction has reached its goal. For these important reasons a good teacher will be fully as much concerned that the pupil has an opportunity to reproduce knowledge as to receive it.

4. Thought-provoking questions

Teaching is more than "hearing lessons," and questions that adequately and permanently instruct must do more than test the pupil's knowledge. They must help the pupil organize and apply his knowledge, and assist him in thinking for himself. They should raise questions as well as secure answers, and certainly stimulate the pupil to know more. A witness in court will be subjected to both direct and cross-examination. His own counsel will seek by questions not only to direct his replies, but his thought as well. In other words, his case can best be furthered by permitting his counsel to think for him. The opposing lawyer, on the other hand, instead of asking him leading questions, by the most rigid examination will compel him to do his own thinking. Indeed, he will have to give all diligence to the barrage of searching questions so that his replies may be accurate and consistent. While his own counsel may *direct* thought, it remains for the opposing attorney to *provoke* thought.

A good teacher, in order to stimulate the thinking of his pupils, will not only need to examine, but to cross-examine them as well. He should prepare thought-provoking questions that involve:

a. Purpose

While the word "what" is used to solicit information, the word "why" should be employed to determine purpose. This is a direct appeal to the reasoning faculties of the pupil, and should be used repeatedly if independent thought is to be encouraged. Our Lord sometimes asked questions to secure information, but usually the facts were elicited to solicit a reason for action. For instance, He struck at the consciences of His critics when He asked, "Is it lawful to do good on the sabbath days, or to do evil? to save life, or to kill?" (Mark 3:4). "Why call ye me, Lord, Lord, and do not the things which I say?" (Luke 6:46).

b. Opinion

Questions which call for personal judgment are of more worth than those which solicit thought that is unrelated to the individual. It is always helpful for pupils to determine in their own minds the relative values of things. Personal judgment was solicited by our Lord by such questions as, "What thinkest thou, Simon?" (Matt. 17:25), and, "Why callest thou me good?" (Matt. 19:17). Many of the questions our Lord asked to strengthen faith were of this character. "Wilt thou be made whole?" (John 5:6); "Believe ye that I am able to do this?" (Matt. 9:28); "Whosoever liveth and believeth on me shall never die. Believest thou this?" (John 11:26).

c. *Application*

Perhaps the most practical type of thought-provoking questions is that which seeks for a personal application of truth. When the lawyer, seeking a debate with our Lord, raised the neighbor question, he was told the story of the Good Samaritan and asked to give his opinion as to which of the three strangers was a true neighbor. It was the lawyer's reply that called forth the divine dictum, "Go, and do thou likewise" (Luke 10:36, 37). The heart-searching question, "Lovest thou me?" that Christ put to Peter, was followed by the command, "Feed my lambs" (John 21:15).

III. PRACTICE OF QUESTIONS

Much of the success in the use of questions depends upon the way they are asked. The teacher must always keep in mind the possibility of a misunderstanding. He ought to consider just how the question will strike the minds of the pupils. "What must we do to have our sins forgiven?" asked a thoughtless teacher. Consequently he was surprised when the pupil replied, "We must first sin." Nevertheless, this was the correct answer from one point of view. If the question had been put in a different form, it would have guided the pupil in giving the answer the teacher desired. Perhaps if the question had been stated, "What must we do, that God may forgive a sin we have committed?" there would have been a clearer understanding.[1]

There are eight principles to be observed in questioning:

1. Avoid reading questions

It hardly need be said that questions must be asked, not read. Although previously prepared in writing, it is well not to bring them to class. Manuscripts and notes are non-conductors of personal interest, and happy is the teacher who can be

[1] Berkeley, *You Can Teach,* p. 39.

independent of them. Nothing should be allowed to come between the teacher and the class during the teaching period.

2. Avoid leading questions

While backward and bashful pupils may be encouraged to participate in the lesson by questions that suggest the answer, it is well to remember that they are not of value either to solicit information or to stimulate thought.

3. Avoid guessing questions

Many questions that can be answered by either "yes" or "no" tempt the pupil to guess rather than to think out the answer. If the pupil does answer "yes" or "no," require proof for the response given. Only as reasons are given can such questions have value.

4. Avoid long questions or double questions

A long sentence is retained in the pupil's mind with difficulty, and he may forget the first part in his effort to grasp the last of it. Eliminate every unnecessary word or phrase, so that the question can be stated as briefly as possible. Long, involved statements are never necessary, and are nearly always confusing.

5. Avoid indefinite questions

Indefinite questioning usually comes from a lack of clear thinking on the part of the teacher. If the original statement is not understood, the answer will of necessity not be clear. Good questions are clear, simple, and direct. Sometimes questions are confusing because they involve more than one answer. Frequently a pupil puzzled between possible answers, will reply promptly when the question is restated in simpler form.

6. Avoid repeating questions and answers

If pupils know that the question will be repeated, the habit of inattention to the first inquiry will develop. For that reason a question should usually not be repeated, but passed on to another pupil who is mentally alert. It is equally unfortunate when the teacher repeats the pupil's answer after him, and thus really recites the lesson. No pupil will put much life into his response if he knows that it is to be immediately reiterated.

7. State question before assigning

Do not name the pupil before asking the question. It only embarrasses him and at once relieves the rest of the class from giving any thought to the interrogation. When the question is stated first, all are obliged to be attentive, since no one knows who will be called on to reply. This is one of the secrets of holding the attention of the class.

8. Assign questions promiscuously

It is a mistake to ask questions in serial order so that each pupil knows just when his turn comes. The element of uncertainty as to whom the teacher will call upon next, is a good incentive to alertness. Restless and mischievous pupils can be arrested by a timely question directed to them.

IV. PROVOKING OF QUESTIONS

One of the surest tests of a teacher's work is found in the questions of his pupils. Find a class that is always asking questions, and you have found a teacher who knows how to awaken minds to the search for truth. The class that is growing, really learning, will be interested. The interested class will ask questions.

Even more important than the question that provokes thoughts is the one that provokes inquiry. There is a double gain in having a pupil express his thoughts. The pupil's question reveals not only his interest, but the readiness of his mind for the instruction. The question is an index that reveals to the teacher the state of the pupil's mind and its stage of development. A question from a pupil often discloses more of his thoughts and more of his needs than would appear through a score of questions from his teacher.

1. Encourage questions

Children love to ask questions. It is to their advantage, and to the advantage of the teacher also, that they should frequently be encouraged to express themselves in this way. People, and especially adults, hesitate to ask questions in a Sunday school class, for fear they will expose their ignorance. Teachers likewise, especially those who are not well acquainted with their class, often refrain from asking questions, lest the result should prove embarrassing. Yet all agree that the quickest and surest way of finding out what is not known is by the simple question and answer method. The child who has been encouraged to be inquisitive is far more likely to ask questions in later years.

2. Answer questions with questions

A high degree of efficiency in the art of questioning has been reached when a teacher is able to answer a question with a question. This throws the responsibility of thought back on the pupil and greatly assists in the realization of that much-to-be-desired aim, of making him an independent investigator. Note how frequently our Lord silenced His critics in this way. When asked on one occasion by what authority He taught and healed, He agreed to reply if they could answer His question regarding John's baptism. This counter question placed our Lord's critics in a dilemma, and they were obliged to admit that they could not reply (Matt. 21:23–27). Other illustrations of counter questioning are found in Matthew 15:2, 3; 22:17–20; Luke 10:25, 26; 14:3–6; 18:18, 19.

Our Lord not only silenced His critics, but also encouraged the questions of His disciples, by asking, "What do you think?" (Matt. 18:12; 21:28; 26:66). In the light of the frequency with which He used this device, one might well ask, "Who should ask more questions, the teacher or the class?" Dr. Dobbins tells of a noted teacher of law, who usually began his class period with the inquiry, "What questions have you?" If no one had a question, the lesson was reassigned and the class dismissed.[2] Teachers ask questions, usually, in order to find out what the pupils do, or do not, know. Pupils ask questions, as a rule, because they face a difficulty which they wish cleared up. Here is an illustration of what the teacher-pupil relationship should be. It is far better for the teacher to confront the class with a problem and challenge them to find its solution, than to present the solution and then test them afterward to see if they have grasped it. It is human nature to move along the line of least resistance, but when teacher and pupils jointly work out the solution of problems the hard way, the result is of permanent and practical value. While the teacher is to constantly stimulate the spirit of inquiry, he must exercise caution in telling his pupils something they can find out for themselves.

QUESTIONS

1. In what respect is the question a teaching weapon or device?
2. Show how our Lord was a master of the art of questioning.
3. State the fourfold purpose of the question.
4. Why should the teacher prepare a list of questions?
5. Name four types of questions.
6. Distinguish between contact and rhetorical questions.
7. Distinguish between factual and thought-provoking questions.
8. Illustrate from our Lord's instruction thought-provoking

[2] Dobbins, *The Improvement of Teaching in the Sunday School*, p. 145.

questions that involve (a) purpose, (b) opinion, and (c) application.

9. Give six things that are to be avoided in asking questions.
10. Make two suggestions regarding the assignment of questions.
11. Why should questions of the pupils be encouraged?
12. Illustrate how our Lord answered a question with a question.

10

Testing

IN OLD texts on pedagogy, the program of the efficient teacher was supposed to be completed when there had been teaching, drilling, and testing. Modern education has eliminated drilling, but still recognizes the importance of testing. In fact, it is safe to say that there is no teaching without testing. Most Sunday school teachers would be surprised to find by any fair testing of their work, how very little, comparatively, has been gained by their pupils. They continue to teach week after week, entirely oblivious to the fact that little of their instruction is being retained by their pupils. The public schools have opened our eyes to this great deficiency in the Sunday school. A questionnaire on Bible facts was given to 850 California high school students, with the following results: 64 per cent of these students did not know that Moses was the world's greatest lawgiver; 83 per cent did not know what Gethsemane is, and why it is famous in Bible history; 78 per cent could not quote two verses from the Bible; 58 per cent could not name five books of the Bible; 48 per cent could not name one writer of the Bible.

Dr. Dobbins gave a test to 81 tenth and eleventh grade high school students in a typical southern town. These students were nearly all regular Sunday school attendants. The questions were purely factual, such as:

Who was the first man?

Name the Pentateuch (the first five books of the Bible).

Who led the children of Israel from Egypt?

Who was the first king of Israel?

Who wrote most of the Psalms?

Name the four Gospels.

Name four of Paul's epistles.

The average grade was 35 per cent! [1]

In one of the public schools of Chicago, a class in the eighth grade was talking about the battle of Waterloo. One of the pupils, in his enthusiasm, spoke of the Calvary charge. Immediately the teacher went to the board and wrote the two words, cavalry, and Calvary. She asked the meaning of the first word. All the pupils knew the answer—armed horsemen. "Now," she said, "here is the word that John used. Tell me what it means to you." There was no reply. Finally one of the boys raised his hand and suggested that it was the name of a cemetery in Chicago. (There is a Calvary Cemetery there.) Another thought it might be the name of a city in Canada (Calgary). The teacher was plainly disappointed. "How many of you boys and girls go to Sunday school?" she asked. Practically every hand was raised. "And do you mean to tell me that you never heard of Calvary? It seems that you would have known the importance of that place in the Bible, if you had known the importance of Waterloo in history, or of New York in geography." It was a revelation to her, and to those whom she told. How little our boys and girls are really learning in Sunday school!

Life itself is constantly testing us. "If teaching is careless, superficial, blundering, the results will be reflected in the failure of our pupils to grasp the truths they should learn, and

[1] Dobbins, *The Improvement of Teaching in the Sunday School,* p. 153.

in the consequent impoverishment of their lives. If our teaching is earnest, thoughtful, skillful, the results will be manifest in the growth and development of our pupils as they incorporate the truths of Christianity in their character and conduct." [2] Sooner or later the teacher's work will be judged, not only of men, but also of God. Those who teach cannot escape the testing of their work.

The methods of testing a pupil's knowledge are quite as simple as the methods of teaching truth. In fact, those who are willing to include a program of testing with their teaching will find that the only difficulty is the inadequacy of the preparation. The first thing for a teacher to consider in the testing process is to impress clearly and permanently in the pupil's mind what he wishes him to remember. Much of the testing may be done by means of

I. THE RECITATION

In a subsequent chapter (17) we shall discover that this is one of our teaching methods. The function of the recitation is primarily to test the knowledge of the pupil. By "testing" this knowledge, we mean "putting it on trial." We submit it to a rigid cross-examination in order to determine whether it is clear or confused knowledge. The test, therefore, needs to be thorough, searching, and inspiring. In testing a pupil's knowledge, the recitation must require full and accurate expression. In no other way can the teacher determine what the pupil knows, and in no other way should he undertake to determine it. Recitation should be free. The pupils should be permitted to say in their own way what they understand to be the truth. They will thus employ their personalities as well as their mentalities in the responses that they make. When a pupil states his views, forms his thoughts and expresses an

[2] Dobbins, *op. cit.,* p. 150.

opinion, the teacher has a look into his soul. That look will reveal to the teacher his duty and obligation.[3]

There are three things that need to be kept in mind when we use the recitation as a means of testing. There must be

1. Preparation for recitation

In the public school, the lesson assigned becomes the basis of recitation at the next class session. Here is an important matter for the Sunday school teacher to ponder. He cannot have a good recitation without proper preparation. Work will have to be assigned in advance of the time when recitation is required.[4] Only with the young children can he dispense with preparation. When pupils come to class without any idea of what the lesson is about, the result is wasted time. Their minds are unprepared. Not only does the teacher find it difficult to make a contact with the lesson, but it is almost hopeless to expect much in the way of recitation.

If we are to depend largely upon recitation as a means of testing, at least five minutes of the class period will have to be spent in assigning work for the following week. Only in this way can we hope that the pupils will come back the following Sunday to recite willingly and intelligently. Before making such assignments, the teacher will have to go over the lesson carefully, in order that only the more important things, those she particularly wishes to be remembered, will have the attention of the pupils while they are preparing.

Pupils need to be guided in their study. That is the purpose of supervised study in public schools. The brevity of the Sunday school period necessitates that this be done at home. But the teacher will have to supervise the study just the same. This can be done in the careful assignments of the parts to be studied.

[3] Martin G. Brumbaugh, *The Making of a Teacher,* p. 165.
[4] Brumbaugh, *op. cit.,* p. 162.

2. Conducting a recitation

Taking for granted that there has been ample preparation through previous study, how is the teacher now to conduct the recitation? There are two methods which may be employed. The first of these is

a. The question method

A skillful questioner is the despair of inadequate preparation. It is also the power that makes clear to the pupil his limitations.[5] By wise use of the question, the teacher may unfold the subject systematically. Of course these questions will not be stereotyped, and to a large extent will be prompted by the response of the pupil. The teacher should arrange questions in such order as to unfold the subject of the lesson in logical sequence. Of course he will not be satisfied with answers of "Yes" and "No." Nor will he predispose the pupil to answer in a manner that would please the teacher, rather than give an opinion of his own.

b. Topical method

The value of the topical method is that there is a good test of expression. It compels the pupil to state a series of connected thoughts, thus throwing upon him the responsibility of organizing these thoughts and of expressing them. For that reason, this method is best suited to more mature pupils. A skillful teacher is required to guide this method of teaching, that it may not degenerate into a discussion unrelated to the topic under consideration. It is perhaps best to combine the question and the topical methods, making use first of one and then the other.[6]

The one supreme purpose of the recitation must be kept in view. It is to test thoroughly what the pupil knows, and what he is able to state concerning what he knows.

[5] Brumbaugh, *op. cit.,* p. 166.
[6] Brumbaugh, *op. cit.,* p. 168.

3. Assigning a recitation

Who shall be called upon to recite, and in what order? There are three plans suggested for making assignments, only one of which is to be recommended.

a. The simultaneous plan

This plan calls for the concert method. The few pupils who are prepared lead in the answers, and the others join in. The teacher has no means of knowing who is talking. In this way the indifferent pupils conceal their inadequate preparation behind the others. This plan should be avoided.

b. The consecutive plan

Some teachers begin at one end of the class, and call upon pupils in regular order. Even some professors in universities and colleges are so lacking in psychological and pedagogical knowledge as to use an alphabetical list for recitation! One day they will begin with the a's, and the next with the z's. Not only does every one know when he going to recite, but there are some pupils who are seldom contacted. The teacher is merely giving individual instruction, since the only pupil who gives close attention is the one who is reciting, and the one who expects to be called upon next.

c. The promiscuous plan

A wise teacher will never give any indication as to which pupils he expects to call on for recitation. The same pupil may be called upon twice in succession, but everyone will be constantly on the alert, as the uncertainty will require that each follow closely the response of the other pupils. Of course, as we have seen in a previous chapter, the assignment is never made to a pupil until after the question has been asked, or the topic has been stated. In the promiscuous method, the teacher may have a plan of making the rounds of the class, so that none will be overlooked, and none will be called upon too frequently; but this plan should be sufficiently complicated so that his procedure cannot be easily detected by the pupils. In other words, the teacher should have a key to his method to which the pupils do not have access.

II. THE EXAMINATION

Examinations are counted essential in all schools but the Sunday school. It is universally understood that if a pupil can in one way or another pass the ordinary class recitations there is no need for any subsequent examinations. But Bible knowledge, if it is worth while, must be obtained and tested by the same method as any other subject.

The word examination has a terror for most people. They recall wearisome cramming for school examinations, the burning of the midnight oil for a hasty review of weeks of instruction, and then the painful ordeal of trying to put on paper what has been laboriously memorized. Many will remember the questions they never anticipated, or the problems they left blank because they were unable to solve them. Teachers and pupils alike have hoped that these wearisome ordeals would not be required in the Sunday school. Yet, if we take our work seriously, if our teaching is earnest, thoughtful, skillful, there will have to be a more exact test than the recitation permits.

One of the limitations of the recitation is that it does not provide an adequate means for the measurement of progress. Something is needed beyond the evidence that the pupil has learned his lesson from day to day. For this reason our public schools, colleges and universities give final examinations. The work of a term, semester, or even a year, is subject to a general review and examination. Personally, I have never favored determining the promotion of a pupil by a final examination. Because of time limitation, an insufficient number of questions are provided for a thorough examination, and the element of chance also enters in, in that the questions submitted might be answered by some who would fail if the teacher had chosen others. Moreover, the physical ordeal of submitting the measurements of a term's work to a single hour is not to be commended, even if there were any mental advantages.

For this reason, in all my classes I have required every student to prepare a term paper, with a bibliography to show his research work. This independent study and expression I have felt should be recognized as of equal worth to the final examination. When there is a plan of testing the daily work, together with a paper, the final examination need not count for more than one-third. Perhaps the best policy for the teacher is to test as he teaches. In that way you will fully comply with all the requirements for testing, and yet will not subject your pupils to the ordeal of final examinations.

We are told in the Bible that children should be brought up "in the nurture and admonition of the Lord" (Eph. 6:4). Nurture means knowledge. Admonition has reference to behavior. There should be examinations in both of these fields.

1. Bible tests

The teacher may ask questions and judge the correctness of the answers, or he may have assigned topics and judge the accuracy of the response. Why not give written tests? [7] The pupils are accustomed to them in the public school. Why not in the Sunday school? The objections, that Sunday school work is on a voluntary basis, and that the Sunday school pupils will resent examinations, is based on the assumption that all tests are burdensome and obnoxious. This is not true. The teacher who is familiar with modern tests, knows that they are really fascinating. They may not be so thorough as the old-fashioned examinations, but they will meet with the pupils' favor.

a. Fields

In the consideration of Bible tests, there are three fields in which the pupil should from time to time be subjected to a final examination.

[7] Dobbins, *op. cit.,* p. 156.

(1). *Historical*

There are historical facts in the narrative of the Bible with which the pupil should be familiar. These can be submitted from time to time for chronological arrangement, and eventually will impress themselves upon the minds of the students. For instance, arrange in order of time the following facts:

> Christ was born in Bethlehem.
> David was the second king of Israel.
> Moses led the Israelites out of Egypt.
> Three thousand were converted at Peter's first sermon.
> Gideon slew a great army with only three hundred men.
> Peter was delivered from prison by an angel.

(2). *Biographical*

In this field, the pupils might be asked, for example, to state one fact in connection with each of the following, after they have arranged the names in the chronological order in which they appear in the Old Testament: Jonah, Miriam, Ahithophel, Esther, Gideon, Jacob, Hannah, Cyrus, Nebuchadnezzar.

(3). *Geographical*

Certain publishing houses, such as Scripture Press, provide outline maps upon which pupils can be required to locate certain cities or places where important events took place. Mimeographed maps can be prepared, tracing them from the original so that an accurate drawing may constantly be before the pupil.

b. *Types*

There are at least four types of tests which pupils undertake spontaneously. In the "Junior Pupil," of the *All Bible Graded Series*,[8] the following true-or-false test appears:

[8] All Bible Graded Series, Scripture Press, Chicago.

(1). True or false

For Luke 2:47–52:

The wise doctors in the Temple were surprised at the wisdom shown in Jesus' answers.

He asked Mary and Joseph, "How is it that ye sought me?"

Jesus said He had to be about His Father's business.

Mary and Joseph did not understand what He told them.

The doctors said, "Stay with us."

Jesus stayed in Jerusalem at the Temple after Mary and Joseph found Him.

Jesus went home with His parents to Nazareth.

Jesus was obedient (subject unto) His parents.

His mother forgot all about what had happened.

Jesus kept growing in wisdom and stature, and in favor with God and man.

(2). Completion

Completion tests are equally interesting, and a little more exacting than the true-false tests, since in the use of the latter the pupil has a 50 per cent chance of guessing right. In the completion tests there are some statements for the pupil to complete in blank spaces left for this purpose. An example appears in the "Junior Pupil," of the *All Bible Graded Series,* where the pupil is required to read II Kings 20:1–3 and take a one-word test by completing each of the following statements with one word:

Hezekiah was sick unto _____.

The prophet who came to see Hezekiah was _____.

Isaiah told Hezekiah that he was going to _____.

Hezekiah sadly turned his face to the _____.

Hezekiah prayed that God would remember he had walked in _____.

As Hezekiah prayed, he _____.

(3). *Multiple choice*

Multiple choice tests offer a wide variety of opportunity to discover what is, or is not, known. An illustration may be found in the Intermediate quarterly of the *All Bible Graded Series.* A geographical test calls upon the pupil to select one of the places given in answer to the question:

Village that didn't see many mighty works because of unbelief? Jerusalem, Nazareth, Capernaum, Bethsaida.

Mountain on which Jesus gave the Beatitudes? Kurn, Hattin, Mt. Olympus, Mt. Hermon, Mt. Zion.

Province through which the Jews hated to pass? Berea, Judea, Galilee, Samaria.

Village where Jesus was always welcome? Bethany, Nazareth, Gergesa, Jericho.

Body of water that obeyed Jesus' command? The Great Sea, Dead Sea, Sea of Galilee, Jordan River.

Region that had a revival because a man told what Jesus did for him? Syria, Decapolis, Caesarea Philippi, Wilderness.

(4). *Matching*

The matching test is one of the most popular with the pupils, since it requires nothing more than the use of lines or numbers. In the following, taken from the "Intermediate Pupil" manual, of the *All Bible Graded Series,* the pupil is told that the short letter to Philemon contains the names of eleven persons. The pupil is requested to match the names with identifying statements, without consulting his Bible, and to draw a line from the name of the character to the statement concerning him.

1. The "brother" whose greeting Paul sent	Paul
	Timothy
2. Runaway slave	Philemon
3. Philemon's wife	Onesimus
4. Philemon's son	Apphia

5. A great missionary in prison	Archippus
6. A rich man of Colosse	Epaphras
7. A fellow-prisoner of Paul	Mark, Aristarchus,
8. Paul's fellow-laborers	Demas, Luke

2. Behavior tests

When our Lord finished His Sermon on the Mount, He said, "Whosoever heareth these sayings of mine, and doeth them, I will liken him unto a wise man, which built his house upon a rock" (Matt. 7:24). The Bible tests have to do largely with the hearing of the Word. Now it is necessary to have the doing also tested. This is not so easily done.

Life consists largely of habitual ways of behavior. A habit is a regular way of thinking, feeling, or acting, that has become more or less automatic through repetition. Children who are to be brought up in the admonition of the Lord need to be assisted in the formation of right habits. The burden of this responsibility lies with the home, but the Sunday school needs to co-operate with the home in the formation of these habits. In these days when drink and divorce have rendered so many children homeless, it is even more necessary for the Sunday school to assume the responsibility of parents.

a. Six point record system

The six point record system is based upon regularity, punctuality, giving, Bible bringing, lesson study, church attendance. The record system based on these six points does not undertake to measure the results in the life of the pupil, but it does record the measure of success or failure with which the habits are being formed. It can be easily seen that if these habits become permanent in the lives of individuals they will be a valuable contribution to Christian character.

b. Character building

Next to winning the pupil to a saving knowledge of the Lord Jesus Christ, "the supreme achievement of Christian education is a well-rounded Christian character. By Christian character, we mean that habits, knowledge, attitudes, choices and conduct are organized around Christ as the center so that all life is under His control. The attainment of this ideal is not instantaneous but progressive. Progress toward it is to be measured by character tests." [9]

"Self-rating scales are popular and useful in helping one discover one's strong and weak points. Just as one looks in a mirror to check up on personal appearance, so one might profitably use a series of questions to determine inner qualities of character." [10]

An illustration of this may be found in the "Intermediate Pupil," of the *All Bible Graded Series*. "Check on your Christian life this week. Day by day during your period of devotions, put a check beside every virtue or vice that represents your actions for that day. Perhaps it will surprise you to see yourself as others see you. Be strictly honest!"

	S.	M.	T.	W.	TH.	F.	S.		S.	M.	T.	W.	TH.	F.	S.
Pride								Humility							
Narrowness								"Bigness"							
Intolerance								Tolerance							
Selfishness								Unselfishness							
Anger								Self-control							
Revenge								Love							
Thoughtlessness								Thoughtfulness							
Impoliteness								Courtesy							
Worrying								Peace							
Grumbling								Joy							
Cheating								Honesty							

[9] Dobbins, *op. cit.,* p. 161.
[10] Dobbins, *op. cit.,* p. 162.

3. Attitude and choice

Important as it is to test habits and knowledge, it is even more necessary to test the outcomes of our teaching in the form of attitudes and choices. The supreme task of the Christian teacher is to shape the immortal destiny of a soul. Each pupil's ultimate decision in the acceptance or rejection of the Lord Jesus Christ is of momentous importance. It is difficult to invent trustworthy instruments for the measurement of the pupil's progress in these spiritual realms. Moreover, regeneration is the work of the Holy Spirit. Who is able to fathom His mysterious operations or know the time when conviction is brought to the heart? But the teacher must be ever alert to use to best advantage that psychological moment when the spirit of inquiry will reveal that the hour of decision in that pupil's life has come, and that he, under God, may be the means of leading this soul to the saving knowledge of his Redeemer.

QUESTIONS

1. How did an examination of high school students prove their ignorance of the Bible?
2. What three things are to be kept in mind in conducting a recitation?
3. Why are assignments necessary for successful recitation?
4. Distinguish between the question and topical methods for conducting a recitation.
5. Which one of the three plans for assigning a recitation could be used and why?
6. Compare the examination with the recitation as a means of testing.
7. In what three fields is it possible to provide interesting exams and why?
8. Name four types of Bible tests.

9. Give an example of the completion test.
10. Compare the multiple choice and the matching test.
11. What is a behavior test?
12. Define and illustrate a character building test.
13. What is meant by tests of attitude and choice?

11

Behavior

GOD is the author of law and order; Satan, of confusion and chaos. Throughout the Bible we see how disorder always accompanied lawlessness. In fact, the word "disciple" means trained in orderliness, and followers of God and disciples of Jesus Christ will be insistent that everything "be done decently and in order" (I Cor. 14:40).

The Bible also declares that "children are to be brought up in the nurture and admonition of the Lord." Nurture is instruction, but admonition is discipline. The word "discipline" comes from "disciple," and it is well to note that our Lord's disciples were "trained in orderliness." If the Sunday school is the training school of the church, its teachers and officers must exercise discipline as well as impart instruction. Moral and spiritual development requires that in addition to being trained to think, pupils must be trained in orderliness.

There is nothing that interferes more seriously with work in the Sunday school than disorder. No real teaching is possible when a class is beyond control. Disorderly pupils frequently more than counteract the efforts of the teacher. Instead of learning obedience, reverence, and the principles of Christian conduct, the class is provided with exhibitions of disrespect for the teacher and disregard for such sacred institutions as God's house, God's Word, and God's day. Children who are quiet and orderly in public school, sometimes throw off all restraints in the Sunday school. They feel that the teacher does not possess the same authority as that exercised by the public school instructor, and take advantage of this fact. To be sure, the Sunday school teacher cannot adopt the authoritative methods in operation in the public school. There is not the degree of authority existing in the Sunday school that is possible in secular instruction. There is no truancy law to compel Sunday school attendance, and it is questionable whether the ban of expulsion can be applied to the unruly pupil. The true mission of the Church, after all, is to hold on to the disorderly member, rather than attempt to get rid of him. But the fact that the methods employed by the public school cannot be adopted by the Sunday school is no excuse for disorder. Pupils can be trained in orderliness, and Christian discipline can be exercised in every Sunday school when teachers and officers once recognize the importance and the means of attaining it.

The problem of discipline may be an occasional one, or it may be continuous. It may involve a single individual, but may also pertain to a class or an entire department. It may be a matter of thoughtlessness or restlessness, or willful and malicious behavior.

There are really not many directions in which we need look for the occasional disorder. Generally we will find that the circumstances, the teacher, or the pupil, is responsible. It is imperative that we locate the exact occasion of the disorder.

I. ORDERLINESS OF THE SCHOOL

Disorder is contagious. One unruly pupil affects another; one distraction leads to another. A disorderly superintendent who proceeds with a poorly prepared program, invites trouble. If pupils find the chairs properly arranged, with songbooks in their places, they will likely leave them that way. A book or paper on the floor is only an invitation for more to follow. An orderly atmosphere is conducive to an orderly pupil. It is well to note how the orderly procedure of everything in a military school contributes to successful discipline. Every officer, meeting strict regulations and moving with predetermined precision, sets a worthy example to the students. Carelessness in attitude and action is a misdemeanor. In the same way, an orderly atmosphere in the Sunday school will command attention and respect. Not only should teachers and officers set a good example, but guard pupils against:

1. Discomforts

The class should be surrounded with as favorable physical conditions as possible. Not infrequently children are placed in chairs adapted for adults and are extremely uncomfortable in them. Their feet cannot reach the floor, and they cannot lean back without partly reclining. The result is wriggling, weariness, and unrest. Sometimes the ventilation is poor, or there are extremes of temperature. When there is no provision made for the wraps, these must be held and handled, and thus prove a disturbing element. The Sunday school pupil ought to be made as comfortable in his Bible study class as he is while studying less important secular subjects in the public school.

Overcrowding means certain disorder. One child, in his effort to make himself comfortable, jostles his neighbor. There is an immediate retaliation. Put two boys in one chair, and usually you will have a fight. Put two girls in one chair, and they'll soon be giggling.

2. Distractions

There is an army of competitives against which a teacher must endeavor to gain and hold the attention of the pupil. To fail is to invite disorder. It is a common thing to find in many Sunday schools a dozen classes grouped in a single room, not far enough apart to keep from interfering with one another. Separate classrooms are the only guarantee that the teacher will have no contender for the attention of his pupils. Curtains, which afford a certain amount of privacy from visual distractions, cannot obliterate the sounds that inform the pupils of what is going on elsewhere.

3. Disturbances

The business of the superintendent is to *protect* the teacher and make it possible for him to accomplish his task under the most favorable circumstances. Instead, however, officers are frequently permitted to interrupt the study of the lesson with collection envelopes or Sunday school literature. These unfortunate interruptions upset both the teacher and the class, and the lesson is seldom resumed without some loss of interest, which may invite disorder. Superintendents should use the same business sense and ability in running a Sunday school as they would apply to any other concern. Their teachers should be as carefully guarded against intrusions and guaranteed as much time and privacy for their work as public school instructors enjoy.

II. ORDERLINESS OF THE TEACHER

The pupil's conduct will be governed by the orderliness of the teacher fully as much as by his surroundings. The teacher will need to be particular about his:

1. Appearance

Any loud or flashy apparel, any extreme of dress which will occasion attention if not comment from the pupils, should be avoided. One can understand why the uniform dress in military circles, as well as in business houses, has its advantages. No individual's garments stand out conspicuously in comparison with those of others.

Any striking mannerism or pronounced peculiarity that

draws attention from the thought of the lesson, may be an indirect means to disorder. The teaching rather than the teacher is expected to occupy the center of the pupil's thought, and when the relative position is reversed, mental if not moral confusion follows.

2. Self-control

Teachers often pray that the Lord will make restless boys and girls quiet and attentive. How many teachers pray for self-mastery? The masterful teacher is the successful one, hence everything that tends to make the teacher lose control of himself should be tabooed. A teacher must first of all learn to control himself. He who cannot control himself is not likely to control others. Many things will try his patience, and he needs to be constantly on his guard lest he become irritated. Pupils recognize the advantages of order and system, but if they discover the teacher in a state of mental confusion, they will disregard the authoritative leadership. Let your authority be covered by all the graces that make pleasant and cordial relationship between teacher and pupil. The calm, quiet, forceful mastery of our Lord, even when His critics tried to irritate Him with hard questions, impressed His listeners and made them all the more eager to hear His words. In every controversy He remained master of the field.

3. Instruction

Not only must the teacher be master of himself, but he must also be master of his subject, if he is to be master of his pupils. Miss Plummer says, "If there is disorder in the class, it is the teacher's fault. The lesson itself should keep order." The poorly prepared teacher should anticipate trouble. Orderliness in instruction prepares for orderliness in conduct. Nothing leads to disorder quicker than inattention, and back of all inattention is disinterest. A poorly prepared teacher is always out of order.

Every teacher who has inattentive pupils should try the experiment of being thoroughly prepared—having enough material to keep every second of the lesson period full of action. Once a teacher tries this plan for holding the attention through uninterrupted instruction, he will very likely be convinced that it is the best solution to any problem of disorder.

4. Tact

Lack of tact leads to disrespect. Call mature boys and girls "children," and you will lose control of them sooner or later. In their own eyes they are not to be classed with the younger generation, and they resent being addressed as juveniles.[1]

III. ORDERLINESS OF THE PUPIL

Disorder is of two kinds, the intentional and the unintentional. The first finds the cause in itself. The second is a result of some other cause. Of four groups of disorderly pupils, only one is to be classified as intentional. In a group there is generally a leader who is the key to the problem. If he can be handled successfully, the others will behave.

1. Thoughtless pupils

A public school teacher not only learns to judge a home by the kind of child who comes from that home, but she recognizes the limited possibility either of neutralizing or of lessening the influence of the home. The Christian teacher in the same way must recognize that certain pupils are thoughtlessly rather than intentionally bad. Even though they may have been taught reverence for sacred things, they are so accustomed to disorder in their homes that they have formed the turbulent habit which constantly wars against their best intentions to comply with the teacher's wishes.

The reverence of Catholics for their institutions does not necessarily reflect any excellence on home government, for

[1] Coleman, *The Romance of Winning Children,* p. 108.

they have similar domestic problems to Protestants. But the Catholic Church better meets the situation by systematic training in the early years of a child's life. In some parishes the parochial school pupil is marched daily into the environment of the church so that reverence for sacred things may be inculcated into his being and become a part of his life. Protestant children need to acquire habits of reverence to make it easy for them to be orderly in Sunday school. If we carefully watch the conduct of the child in the Beginners and Primary departments, and his regular attendance at the sessions, it should be natural for him to be well behaved in the subsequent departments.

2. Restless pupils

While the thoughtless pupil may be the victim of an unfortunate environment, the restless pupil owes his shortcomings to his heredity. Many boys and girls are by nature restless, but this should not be considered a liability. It is true that "some boys don't go wrong because they don't go at all," and it is possible to be "so good as to be good for nothing." Robert Louis Stevenson said, "Give me the boy who has brains enough to make a mistake." The average boy is an active creature. He delights in doing something, and if his teacher cannot keep him employed, he will usually be able to supply the entertainment himself. Of course, the remedy for this type of pupil is a full program of activities. The teacher who insists upon doing all of the talking is sure to have competition. Only insofar as the restless pupil is given an opportunity to participate in the lesson can there be any assurance that he will be docile. While the teacher will not overlook the "quiet" member of the class who also "learns by doing," nevertheless the active pupil will need a major portion of the assignments so that all may benefit by the instruction. The reason the Daily Vacation Bible school has been able to control restless boys and girls successfully for a period twice the length of the Sunday school, during the hot weeks of summer, is that the large program of expressional work particularly fits their needs. Graded lesson material, with ample provision for the pupils' activities, will be a great aid to the Sunday school teacher in meeting this type of disorder.

3. Self-centered pupils

These include the "spoiled" child, who is accustomed to having his own way at home—and at school if possible. It is difficult for him not to occupy the stage, at least part of the time, and his contribution will not always harmonize with the lesson. Such a self-assertive pupil needs to be "taken down," but it is not always easy for the teacher to know how to go about it. Miss Plummer relates what one teacher did when one of her pupils blew a whistle in class:

> "The teacher said, 'Why, Johnny has a whistle. A whistle is a very good thing. What is a whistle good for?' The interest of the teacher seemed so genuine that several were encouraged to reply, in spite of Johnny's red face. Then the application was skillfully made. The calls of the Bible, the warnings, the admonitions were referred to as God's manner of attracting attention. Quick as a flash came the thought, the Bible says, 'Blow the trumpet in Zion'—a whistle blown for God's people, a warning we should all heed. The theme was developed helpfully. In the course of the diversion the teacher wanted to see the whistle, took it in her hand, commented a bit on its construction, and kept it until the completion of the lesson, in which were found some 'whistle warnings' of value." [2]

Generally the self-centered pupil can be successfully reprimanded by the ridicule of his companions, and will be prop-

[2] Plummer, *The Soul-Winning Teacher,* p. 71.

erly subdued if the laugh is turned against him. Public opinion as expressed on the playground is a respected teacher. The child who always wants to be "it," is soon taught by the consensus of his companions that selfishness and stubbornness mean exile. The penalty of ostracism decreed by this juvenile court is an effective school for the spoiled child. Excessive egotism may avail with a foolish, fond mother, but it is ruled out by the court of public opinion. For this reason the self-centered child should constantly be exposed to the leveling process of his playmates, who can more effectively punish the sin of self-assertiveness than the teacher. Such pupils have not played or mingled widely with other children probably.

4. Malicious pupils

Boys and girls who come to Sunday school to instigate mischief and whose evil bent is sufficiently recognized by their companions as to constitute leadership, provide a real problem for the teacher. It is doubtful if much is to be gained by methods employed to suppress those whose disorder is intentional. Interest and activity that might divert others from mischief may fail here, and we can no longer depend on the lesson itself to keep order. This does not mean that the teacher is to be imposed upon or permit one unruly member to spoil the lesson period. He will have to be firm in his dealing with such a character. And he can be firm and forceful without losing patience and becoming indignant or even sarcastic. Such action only reflects upon the Christian character of the instructor and acccomplishes nothing with this type of pupil. The teacher who scolds will never be respected or imitated, and the pupil who is scolded will evince his humiliation by a bravado of manner intended to impress his classmates with his indifference. Kindly and yet firmly the disorderly pupil should be reprimanded, and if the admonitions are not respected, it may be necessary to request him to withdraw. Before reaching such a climax, however, the teacher should plan to make friendly contact with him during the week. More than one obstreperous boy has been conquered by a persevering teacher who took time to visit him, discover his interests, and win his confidence.

John was full of mischief. He was never happy unless he was making faces or playing some prank. His Sunday school teacher complained to the superintendent that she could do little with him, or with the class, for he kept it in a constant uproar with his amusing performances. "Look at him now!" she said to the superintendent. Sure enough, in the center of a group of grinning boys, his facial contortions and comical antics were a source of great enjoyment. "That's the monkey," said the superintendent, as he went down to see what he could do with him. He grabbed the boy by the collar and shook him lively, while he told him that the Sunday school was no place for monkeys, and that if he did not keep quiet and behave himself he would have to be put out of the school.

Immediately the boy straightened himself and sat in sullen, obstinate silence. Not a word could his teacher get out of him, and he sat that way throughout the rest of the hour. When she spoke to the superintendent about his obstinacy, he said, "That's the mule." However, he resolved to call at the boy's home and have a talk with the mother. He went the next morning when he thought the boy would be in school, but imagine his surprise when, in a dilapidated little house, he found this boy at the washtub helping his mother.

"I have come to see you about John," he said.

"Oh!" said the mother, tears filling her eyes, "I don't know what I would do without him. Since his father died he has helped me with my washings, which are our only means of support. My health is so poorly that were it not for him, I do not know what I would do."

The superintendent did not say what he had intended to say. Instead he remarked, "There, that's the man."

In every boy there is the monkey and the mule, but there is also the making of a man. In fact, the combination of these two characteristics will manifest itself in the formation of a manly character. A boy who is all monkey will never be anything more than a silly child, and a boy who is all mule will never rise above the level of a sullen beast; but the contribution of both monkey and mule in their combination will produce the man.

QUESTIONS

1. Show how the word "disciple" is related to orderliness.
2. Compare the difficulties of maintaining order in Sunday school and in public school.
3. Contrast the disorderly conduct of some Sunday schools with that of a military academy.
4. What three things contribute to the disorder of a school?
5. How may a superintendent prevent distractions and disturbances?
6. In what three ways may the teacher contribute to good order?
7. Why is self-control so important for maintaining good order?
8. Name four types of disorderly pupils.
9. Discuss the thoughtless pupil and how his need may be met.
10. How should the problem of the restless pupil be met?
11. What can be done with the self-centered pupil?
12. Suggest a plan for dealing with the malicious pupil.

Part IV: *The Lesson*

12

Assembling Material

MARION LAWRANCE said: "The greatest need in our church work today is trained teachers who will put their whole mind into their preparation, their whole souls into their presentation, and their whole life into their illustration." Such a teacher will not be satisfied with a hurried preparation Saturday evening for the next day's lesson. A trained teacher will realize that more exercise of his faculties than that will be necessary to keep him in training. Poise in the presence of his class, which so conspicuously marks a trained teacher, cannot be maintained without the mastery of the lesson of the day and a reserve knowledge of the Bible and its truths. Dr. A. H. McKinney inquires:

"Are we not seeking to learn how the teacher may have that poise during the lesson study period which gives him the mastery of the situation? It may not be easy to gain such poise, but it is well worth paying a large price in order to obtain it. What is the price? Prepare carefully every lesson you are to teach. Get the largest possible acquaintance with the contents of the Bible as a whole, with its historical, geographical, and social background, with the truths which it imparts. Having done this, you will have made much progress toward the poise which is so desirable and so essential in successful teaching." [1]

[1] McKinney, *A Top-Notch Teacher,* p. 90.

The value of the time and opportunity afforded by the Sunday school hour should be appreciated. It is a brief time at best. How important then, that every precious moment shall be turned to the best possible account. Observation shows unmistakably that there is no greater cause for a waste of recitation time than a feeling of unpreparedness on the part of the teacher. Not having a definite plan for beginning causes hesitation, apology and delay. The Christian teacher can learn something from the methods of the most successful school teachers, who painstakingly prepare for each recitation. They know they must do this if they are to hold the attention of the thinking, progressive pupils.

In a previous lesson we studied the preparation of the teacher. Now attention should be given to the preparation of the lesson. This will consist largely of the assembling and organizing of lesson material. The first part of this important phase of a teacher's work will be considered in this lesson, and the second part in a subsequent study. In the assembling of lesson material, the first consideration should be its sources.

I. THE SOURCE OF MATERIAL

1. Bible

The Bible is the textbook of the Bible school, therefore it should be the teacher's first study. Aside from the fact that it is the inspired Word of God, it is the recognized text of the school which entitles it to first consideration. When one uses lesson helps exclusively, he is apt to appropriate the thoughts of others and do no original thinking himself. Lesson helps should be used with the Bible and never apart from it. The plan of printing Scripture with the helps has been a temptation for teachers and pupils to dispense with the Bible. The new *All Bible Graded Series* of Sunday school lessons has not made this mistake, as its helps are unintelligible without the accompanying Textbook. Every true teacher knows that the Bible is its own best interpreter, and that by comparing scripture with scripture infallible light is thrown on obscure passages. At this point it might be well to recognize that the supplementary content of Bibles is of three kinds. The first is serviceable for

a. Information

Some Bibles contain many valuable geographical, historical, and archæological helps, but as these can all be provided in other volumes, such a type of Bible is not of the first importance.

b. Interpretation

A few Bibles are now offered with copious notes and comments on various passages. In reality a commentary is provided with the text. Such explanations are valuable, especially to a beginner, but they have the effect of discouraging independent thinking and of tempting the student to accept the opinion of the commentator as his own.

c. Investigation

The great aim of the teacher, as we have already seen, is to make the pupil an independent investigator of truth. That will not be possible unless he himself is an investigator. To that end the best kind of a text will be a chain reference Bible, or one amply supplied with references, so that parallel passages can be independently investigated and Scripture compared with Scripture. Bibles of this character in the hands of adolescent pupils will make it possible for them to be profitably employed in hunting parallel passages and related incidents and teachings for further illustration of the truth which is being studied. The class period may become a real Scripture-searching hour, and the pupils can acquire skill in using their Bibles to find help for themselves as it may be needed.

2. Bible dictionary

If a teacher can possess only one book in addition to the Bible, that volume should be a Bible dictionary, which is in reality a topical Bible, as it gathers from all parts of Scripture every reference pertaining to a particular subject.

3. Bible concordance

Some Bibles are provided with a concordance, but they are abbreviated so that one is often disappointed in not finding the word that will direct him to the desired passage. Strong's, Cruden's, or Young's complete concordance will serve every purpose.

4. Bible commentary

After he has carefully investigated the passages of Scripture designated for the lesson, the teacher will want to know what interpretation and explanation Bible scholars give to difficult verses. Dr. James M. Gray's *Christian Worker's Commentary* is an excellent one-volume work of this kind, while a complete set of Jamieson, Fausset and Brown is to be recommended for those who desire a more exhaustive commentary. Books of this type are so valuable that the school may well afford to provide them for a church library and to make them available at all times for the use of their teachers.

5. Lesson helps

In studying the lesson from the Bible, read it specifically: First, for the story; second, for the incidents; third, for the persons mentioned; and fourth, for the practical teachings. Then when lesson helps are finally consulted, the teacher will see a great deal more in them than otherwise because he is getting light on what he has already covered in his Bible reading and study. He will discover that he has already thought of many things mentioned in the lesson help, and he will have the satisfaction of blazing a way for himself. Lesson helps should supplement the teacher's knowledge. Sometimes a difficult passage is made clear or an apt illustration is provided. Sometimes the helps provide some information on oriental manners and customs that is essential to a right understanding and application of the Scripture passage.

6. Maps

Children of school age should be as familiar with Bible geography as with that of their own country. It will not be possible for them to follow the journeys of the patriarchs, the wanderings of Israel, or the campaigns of Joshua and David without the aid of maps. If maps found in the ordinary Bible are the only ones available, these should be studied with much care. Wall maps, especially those constructed by the members of the class, are the most practical and profitable.

7. Pictures

Teachers of children have long recognized the value of visual instruction; pictures should be collected from various sources not only to illustrate but also to present the truth more vividly. As some of the greatest works of art are Bible scenes, copies of suitable masterpieces should be made available for instruction. Hundreds of such pictures hang in our art galleries, and not a few of them have been incorporated into several excellent series for the Sunday school.

II. THE SELECTION OF MATERIAL

Someone has said that in the selection of lesson material we should go to:

(1) The Bible for all things.

(2) Books for past things.

(3) Newspapers for present things.

(4) Human nature for point of contact.

A teacher, like the reporter of a newspaper, should be constantly on the alert for lesson material in his devotional study, in his reading of books, magazines, and newspapers, in listening to the radio, and in personal contacts. But in the gathering of promising material the teacher should:

1. Provide for future lessons

A carefully planned series of lessons, like the *All Bible Graded Series,* is not made up of independent units. As in the study of geography, history, mathematics, or any secular subject, each lesson is related to those preceding and those following in such a way as to develop a theme which runs through the entire series. In such a series of lessons one lesson cannot be taught apart from those before and after it. Instead of gathering material merely for the next lesson, the teacher will have in mind all the lessons that present a general theme, and these may cover an entire quarter.

If the teacher is to have the class participate, it is quite necessary that the lesson be assigned the previous Sunday. And if these assignments are to be made with the care and the effectiveness they deserve and are to secure the co-operation of the pupils, the teacher will have to give considerable time and study to an advanced lesson. When we remember that Sunday school lessons written for religious papers must be prepared from four to six weeks before they are published, the manuals of the *All Bible Graded Series,* six months in advance, and such annual periodicals as *Peloubet's Select Notes,* more than a year before the lessons are used, it will be seen that the consideration of future lessons is neither impossible nor impractical.

2. Provide for individual needs of pupils

As material is selected, the teacher will keep in mind not so much the class as the individuals of his class. In the teaching of the lesson Sunday after Sunday the teacher cannot fail to discover the needs of his pupils, and as a fond father will search for some suitable gift that will meet the needs and desires of his son, so a teacher will ever be on the watch for material that will best meet the needs of each pupil. This will be true not only of instruction that may be imparted, but of what the pupils may themselves discover from personal research or assignment in which they have been directed by the teacher.

3. Provide for personal needs of teacher

In our study of the preparation of the teacher, we stressed the importance of reading constantly, systematically, and intelligently, in order to be mentally alert. The teacher may be a channel through which streams of helpful instruction may constantly flow to the pupils, if he is wisely tapping reservoirs that will enrich his own life. The teacher, who is constantly on the lookout for those things that will enlarge his vision, increase his knowledge, and deepen his spirituality, will have the satisfaction of seeing his pupils drink from a running brook rather than a stagnant pool.

III. THE SAVING OF MATERIAL

As the human mind does not, except in rare instances, remember half of what it sees or hears, some provision should be made for conserving worthwhile material.

1. Paint mental pictures

Before the teacher can bring the facts vividly before the imagination of the pupils, he must have them distinctly before his own imagination. He cannot make the pupils see what he himself does not see. For this reason, promising lesson material should be reproduced in mental pictures. As ninety per cent of imagination is memory, the teacher in reading newspapers, magazines, or books, should stop frequently, close his eyes and strive to form a vivid picture of the scene and of the persons about whom he has just been reading. Let the teacher try this experiment on himself and endeavor to discover how much visualizing power he possesses. As a child recalls an object of his construction far better than something of which he has only seen or heard, so the construction of these mental pictures will provide a permanent impression for the future use of the teacher. Power to see these new pictures vividly, as well as to use the imagination with ease and rapidity, will come with practice and cultivation of this wonderful faculty of the mind.

2. Provide a notebook

Writing assists the memory in retaining information, and keeping a record preserves it for future use. Such a depository of teaching material should be kept:

a. *For general information*

One should not read without thinking, and one should not think without writing. If on reflection the teacher has discovered something worthwhile for his class, he should either copy it in the notebook or note the book and page so that it can be readily found when needed. The notebook should—

(1). *Record facts*

Statistics of all kinds are valuable for the foundation as well as the court of appeal for class discussion. Statements of representative men also will carry authority. The latest discoveries and inventions may be found useful in making a point of contact with a wide-awake class.

(2). *Record experiences*

True stories of human experience are always interesting, and more of these are in the religious realm than most people imagine. Remarkable answers to prayer and other miracles of God's providence are constantly being reported, and a teacher can always make effective use of them, especially if the experience is closely related to some member of the group.

(3). *Record illustrations*

The value of illustrations in the teaching of the lesson has already been stressed, so that every teacher will want to have a large fund in his possession. To one who is on the alert, illustrations will readily suggest themselves from nearly every source of material, but unless notation is made at the time, they will be forgotten. Only by taking notes and referring to them when preparing the lesson is it possible to preserve most of the illustrations from daily life for future use.

b. For specific lessons

The notebook should also be used for a comprehensive forward look over the lesson. Perhaps it is sufficient if provision is made for the thirteen lessons of each quarter, although Amos R. Wells believed that there should be at least fifty-two pages, one for each lesson of the year. Mr. Wells says:

"Head each page with the title of the lesson and the Scripture reference, and use these blank pages for planning your teaching far ahead. If you are a wise teacher, you will be always on the lookout for teaching material. Every walk through the woods gives you a teaching parable. Every copy of the newspaper gives you an illuminating incident from current history. Every book brings you a fine anecdote or appealing thought. Every day your observation of the men and women around you is rich in illustrative material. Much of this is entirely unsuited to the immediate Sunday school lesson, and will be lost unless you have this storehouse in which to garner it, placing it under that lesson with which it seems most appropriate." (cf. How to Teach in Sunday School. Theodore E. Schmauk.)

The chief value of the notebook to the teacher will be in the cultivation of the habit of thinking ahead over the lessons to come. Until this plan has been tried, the teacher will have little idea how this survey of the entire lesson series strengthens the presentation of the individual lesson. If he faithfully uses his notebook, he will soon come to regard it as his chief pedagogical aid.

QUESTIONS

1. Name seven sources of lesson material.
2. a. What three types of Bibles are available?
   b. Which is the most valuable for research work?

3. For what four objects should lessons be studied from the Bible?

4. How should lesson helps be used?

5. Why are maps and pictures to be included as essential lesson material?

6. For what threefold purpose must all lesson material be selected?

7. Why does a series of lessons require advance preparation?

8. As material for the lesson is selected, who should be kept in mind?

9. In what way can the teacher provide for his personal needs?

10. Show the value of reproducing material in mental pictures.

11. a. What is the value of a notebook?

   b. What three lines of general information should be kept in it?

12. What provision in the notebook should be made for specific lessons?

13

Organizing Material

MANY have the impression that the preparation of the lesson is complete when sufficient material has been secured to "fill in the time." It is an unpardonable weakness for any teacher to "mark time" while waiting for the closing bell; he has something more to do than simply to "keep going."

It is a common mistake to imagine that a religious lesson requires less preparation than a secular one. Indeed, there is much to be learned from successful school teachers who painstakingly prepare for each recitation. In the teaching of every class someone must suffer. If the teacher does not suffer before the lesson begins, the pupils are apt to suffer afterward. Teaching is real work.

Lesson material must be organized. There must be a process of elimination as well as accumulation. It is the teacher's business to complete his lesson. He may not be able to teach all there is to teach, but he should complete all that he has planned to teach, and his material should be organized with that in mind. Lesson material may be said to be well organized when it is outlined and fitted into the lesson period. The value and opportunity of the golden hour of the Sunday school must be fully appreciated. It is a solemn responsibility. The lesson material must be selected with the pupils in mind as well as

175

the time at our disposal. There is more than one way to organize lesson material.

I. METHODS OF ORGANIZING MATERIAL

Dr. George Herbert Betts points out four different methods of organization used in preparing material for teaching.

1. Haphazard organization

The haphazard plan, which is really no plan at all, is all too common among teachers today. It indicates either a lack of preparation or a lack of ability, and neither of these will be found in a well-trained teacher. We have all listened to addresses, and even sermons and lectures, which were constructed after the haphazard plan. It was difficult either to follow or to remember them. If our pupils cannot see that we have a clear understanding of the lesson and have arranged its materials in an orderly way, there will be confusion of thought, dullness of perception, and dimness of impression.

2. Logical organization

This consists of sorting out the material and selecting only that which can be appropriately related in the development of the lesson. The different parts of the subject matter must be fitted together in the way best suited to its logical relationships. It recognizes the all-important law of apperception and constantly proceeds in the arrangement of facts from the known to the unknown, for there must be logical thinking on the part of the pupil fully as much as on the part of the teacher.

3. Chronological organization

The element of time enters so fully into our thinking, and such a large portion of the Bible consists of a series of facts which can best be grasped and retained when unfolded in their historical relationship, that this method can be used to great advantage. God's revelation to man was progressive. By this we mean that He did not impart in the beginning a full knowledge of Himself, or completely disclose His plan concerning man. It was only as the centuries passed that He unfolded more and more of His divine purpose to those chosen writers who recorded His Word. For this reason, chronological organization will need to be kept in mind not only in preparing a distinct lesson, but also in planning the entire curriculum of Bible study.

4. Psychological organization

This method consists of planning the subject matter to fit the mind and needs of the child. It must be reiterated that the subject matter must be within the grasp and understanding of the pupil. If it cannot be adapted to his comprehension, or applied to his experience, it must be discarded. There is no virtue in presenting truths, however significant and profound, if they are beyond the reach of the pupil's experience. Material which is not adapted to the understanding is soon forgotten; or if retained, it weighs upon the intellect and dulls its edge for further learning. "We dare not forget the child when we teach religion." [1]

Modern educators lay great stress on the psychological organization of materials—some do it to the exclusion of every other method. Its weakness, like the experience mode of procedure, is in its departure from the Bible as the content of instruction, and its primary stress on application rather than on acquisition of God's Word. It is true that we dare not "forget the child" when we teach, but it is also true that we dare not forget that the Bible is the only authoritative revelation that will enable us to teach the truths of Christianity. To have our lesson material Bible-centered does not mean that we ignore the age and understanding of the pupil. In one sense of the word, all teaching material should be submitted to the psycho-

[1] Betts, *How to Teach Religion,* p. 130.

logical test of its appropriateness to the age and understanding of the pupil. But we never can apply a psychological test to the *value* of God's Word; what may be rejected as unsuitable or too advanced on one occasion must be utilized on another. While in the Beginners and Primary departments a psychological organization of material may have first consideration, the chronological is better for the Junior and Intermediate departments, and the logical for young people and adults.

II. STEPS IN ORGANIZING MATERIAL

1. Aim of instruction

The entire preparation will center around the aim or purpose to which the teacher must determine resolutely to adhere in the presentation of the lesson. All of the assembled material will have to be examined in the light of this purpose. In making a preliminary survey of what has been gathered for the next lesson, the teacher should ask, "What can I find here that will meet some real need in the lives of my pupils?" The answer of this question will provide the teacher with the real aim of the lesson. Do not be satisfied with the aim of the writer who prepares the lesson helps for your department. The writer can only make suggestions from the *content* of the lesson. The teacher can better determine his aim from the *conduct* of his pupils. Does the lesson teach faith, or obedience, or love, or duty to God or to man? Does it suggest such Christian graces as humility, kindness, generosity? Does it encourage Bible study, prayer, or Christian fellowship? Does it deal directly or indirectly with God's plan of salvation? How then can it be made definitely to touch the life of each member of the class? Decide what your class needs and what they should receive from this lesson. Run over in your mind the various pupils that constitute your class and see what particular individuals among them you are going to reach in a helpful way. Such a knowledge will give not only definiteness to your aim but appropriateness to your method and application.

2. Methods employed

The age of the pupils will determine largely the methods to be employed; but there are other factors to be considered. A good teacher will probably select several methods in order to make an effectual presentation of the lesson. The organization of the material will have an important bearing on this selection. Much more material will be required for the lecture than the discussion method, and more time will be needed for the reports of assignments than when the teacher takes the leading part in the discussion. If questions are to be used extensively, not nearly as much ground will be covered. All of these circumstances peculiar to the methods employed will have an important bearing in ascertaining how much material can be used in the allotted time. The character of the lesson will also determine its treatment. The conquests of Joshua, or the journeys of Paul, for example, will call for visual instruction, or maps.

3. Material used

The aim and method having been determined, the teacher will wish to make a careful study of all the available helps. The teacher should prepare more material than is required so that he can feel at ease. At the same time, there must be careful selection and elimination. Not all the material provided even in lesson helps can be used by any one teacher, and he must select that material which will most definitely help in the realization of the aim in mind. After years of teaching experience, Amos R. Wells wrote: "Learn to simplify your teaching and focus it more upon a few facts and truths. As I remember it, I used to put enough into each half hour for two full hours. The result must have been to confuse my pupils and fill them with dismay. My teaching was all lectures, though usually under the thin disguise of questions and answers. Thus I was all the time pouring into baskets full of holes. If I had to do it over, I would think less of what I was giving, and more of what the pupils were getting." [2]

Taking into consideration the extra time required for the report of assignments and the development of the lesson through questions, the teacher will arrive at approximately the proper amount of material that can be used in the allotted time. This will include the Bible passages, memory work, pictures, or any collateral material to be considered.

4. Lesson outlined

The teacher, as well as the preacher, needs to arrange an outline of three or more divisions. For inexperienced teachers, the making of this division will be difficult, and at first they may use the outlines prepared by others in lesson helps. With study and experience, however, they will learn to construct their own division heads—a much better practice than using a ready-made outline.

The outline should provide for several general divisions, or topics, with minor points, illustrations and applications grouped under them. The ease, effectiveness, and conclusiveness with which the lesson is developed will depend largely on the perfection of this outline. Facts should be listed under the topic or division to which they are related and in the order of their importance. If pressed for time, the teacher can then concentrate his attention in the concluding minutes, on the main heads of the outline, omitting the secondary topics. Following this plan, the teacher will not be caught by the closing bell, with the lesson only half presented. Moreover, after a little experience, a good instructor will learn not to introduce

[2] Schmauk, *How to Teach in Sunday School*, p. 282.

a topic in his outline which he cannot at least touch upon in the teaching of the lesson.

5. Questions prepared

While the best questions will depend upon the response of the pupils and therefore cannot be prepared in advance, it is well to have a set of pivotal questions thought out and set down for guidance. If the lesson is to be developed largely by the use of questions, it is necessary that the greater facts and truths be brought into prominence, and that the pupils recognize the pathway of thought and feel that they are making progress on it as the lesson proceeds. Writing out questions in advance also helps to formulate that type of inquiries that will be thought-provoking and free from those errors that reduce the effectiveness of the question.

6. Illustrations selected

We have observed in a previous lesson that a teacher cannot depend on an appropriate, spur-of-the-moment illustration. It must be selected and introduced in the outline beforehand. Some teachers begin the lesson with an illustration drawn from the everyday experience of the pupil, to attract attention on the one hand, and to impress the truth, on the other hand. This illustration may then be referred to throughout, and especially at the close of, the teaching period, for the purpose of showing its bearing on the truth taught. It is well to examine the lesson outline to ascertain what point needs to be made clearer, then to seek to illustrate from common experiences of life, from nature, from history, by story or song. Do not over-illustrate, and thus eclipse rather than illuminate the central truth.

7. Applications suggested

If we have been pupil-minded as we assembled and organized our material, this important part of the preparation will not be difficult. "How am I to impress upon my pupil's mind the truth which I want him to express in his daily living?" is the pertinent question that every teacher must frequently ask during his preparation. He must ever keep in mind the various individuals of his class and what they most need, or what will be most helpful to the class as a whole.

8. Pupil's co-operation

There is no part of the preparation that needs more thought than this. Training one's pupils is more difficult than teaching them. More skill is required to lead a pupil to learn something by his own study than to teach him something. In fact, one needs ever to remember that the real task of the teacher is *to make the pupil an independent investigator of truth.* A definite task for each pupil should be thought out in advance. The pupil's co-operation is to be kept in mind in all

a. Research work

The making of assignments for the next lesson is one of the main secrets of securing effective co-operation on the part of the pupil. These assignments should be:

(1). Definite

It is not enough to urge boys and girls to "study the lesson." Many times the pupil tries to do this, but not knowing *how* to study, is overwhelmed and discouraged at the size of the task. Give him something definite to do. Miss Plummer has given twelve excellent suggestions for definite home work.[3] It is also essential that the teacher be definite in assigning the sources of help. Pupils need to know just what books to consult, and usually it is well to put the material in their hands, with an offer to help them in their research.

(2). Individual

Assignments should be not only definite but individual. For instance, one pupil should have this question to look up;

[3] Plummer, *The Soul-Winning Teacher*, p. 99.

another, this topic to report on; a third, this map to draw; a fourth, these Bible references to compare. The interest, capacity, and ability of the pupil will largely determine the nature of the assignment. Every member of the class should be included if possible.

b. Class work

Aside from such research work as may be assigned to the pupil to prepare at home, there will need to be very definite plans made for his presentation of this work during the class session.

(1). Questions

In the preparation of the questions to be used in class, thought must be given to the interests of the pupils not only to be assured of a response, but to "draw them out" to express themselves freely on the lesson.

(2). Topics

Where the class has a background of Bible knowledge, or will make a real study of the lesson, topics may be assigned to individual pupils to introduce a general discussion. The class will generally feel more free to join in a discussion introduced by one of their own number, than one presented by the teacher. Care will have to be exercised in making the assignments so that the pupil may be depended upon to make a hearty response; failure here may make it difficult to get others to co-operate. It is not well to begin with the timid or backward pupils, but they will be likely to follow after the more assuming ones have participated.

(3). Teaching

In the older classes, sometimes it is possible for one of the pupils to teach the lesson. However, while this is excellent experience for the instructor, frequently it does not work out so well for the other members of the class. Therefore it is probably best to limit the responsibility of the pupils to the presentation of a particular portion of the lesson.

QUESTIONS

1. What is the difference between assembling and organizing material?
2. Name four methods of organizing material.
3. a. Distinguish between the logical and chronological methods.
   b. State for what departments they are best suited.
4. a. What is the weakness of the psychological method?
   b. In what department is its use permissible?
5. State the eight steps in organization of material.
6. What attention should be given to the aim of the lesson?
7. Name two circumstances that will determine the methods to be employed.
8. Make some suggestions as to the amount of material necessary.
9. How should the teacher proceed in making an outline?
10. Discuss the introduction of questions, illustrations, and applications.
11. What provisions should be made for the home work of the pupils?
12. What plans should be made for the pupils' co-operation in class?

14

Illustration

W E HAVE already seen that the illustration is nothing more than a retreat to familiar ground, and as such, constitutes an important part of the law of apperception. The pupil can learn the new only in terms of the old, so that when the advance is more rapid than the mind can follow, the illustration is introduced as a temporary retirement to known scenes in order that the lagging understanding may catch up.

I. VALUE

The importance of illustrations in teaching cannot be over-emphasized. Popular preachers and platform speakers are usually masters of the art of illustrating, but few Sunday school teachers realize the value of illustrations sufficiently to cultivate skillful use of them. Since nothing new can be learned except in terms of the old, the teacher's work is not done when he has presented the facts of a lesson. If they are beyond the mental capacity of his pupils, little progress has been made. In fact, disorder and disinterest most frequently arise from a hazy understanding, which could quickly be clarified by an illustration. It was not the remarkable voice he possessed or the depth of thought he expressed so much as his vivid illustrations that enabled Dr. Spurgeon to hold multitudes spellbound. This great preacher in his talk to teachers said:[1]

"I am sure if I were a boy listening to some of you, unless you told me a tale now and then, you would as often see the back of my head as my face. I don't know, if I sat in a hot schoolroom and you did not strive to interest me, but that my head would nod and I would go to sleep, or be playing with Tom on my left. So don't forget to give your pupils a few anecdotes. Wherever you go, if you are really a good teacher, you can always find something to make into a tale to tell your children. A dear child once said, 'Father, I like to hear Mr. So-and-so preach, because he puts some "likes" into his sermons—"like this and like that."' Yes, children always love those 'likes.' Make parables, pictures, and diagrams for them, and you will always get on."

The large use of illustrations by such an eminent preacher should convince all that they are not merely for little children. Our Lord in dealing with adults frequently employed illustrations. That oft-occurring phrase, "the kingdom of heaven is like unto," suggests His recognition that the new instruction needed to be illustrated with the light of familiar scenes. How frequently He found material in nature and in human life, that served so excellently to clarify His instruction! Turning to the Old Testament, one is impressed with the frequent employment of illustrations by the prophets. To clarify truth Jeremiah used the girdle, the bottle, and the potter's vessel; Ezekiel, the roll, the tile, the beard; Amos, the locust, the plumbline, the summer fruits; Zechariah, the myrtle trees, the measuring line, the candlestick. A striking object lesson was necessary before Peter could be brought to understand that God did not want his prejudices to stand in the way of his ministry to the Gentiles (Acts 10:9–16).

All of these instances of the use of the illustration are impressive. They place its value beyond dispute, and we are justi-

[1] Charles Haddon Spurgeon, *Teaching Children*, p. 355.

Illustration 187

fied in making this device an important part of the teacher's equipment. However, a word of warning needs to be sounded at this point. Important as is the illustration, its value is lessened if it is overdone. It is unfortunate when through a wrong emphasis the story is remembered and the truth it illustrates is forgotten. Better one or two striking illustrations that will remain in the mind of the pupil and will recall the truth to be expressed in his life, than a number which are simply remembered for the interest they aroused. Just as too much light dazzles the eye and impedes the vision, so also many illustrations may confuse perception and hinder thought.

II. VARIETY

The field of illustrations is a large one. One will be astonished at the many ways in which this important factor in teaching may be employed. There are, however, two general divisions.

1. Visual

We are so accustomed to thinking of Sunday school teaching as talking that it is well to be reminded how much information a pupil receives through the eye-gate. Not only do children remember far better what they see than what they hear, but they also comprehend such instruction more easily and more quickly. For this reason it is easy to see that of those two modern agencies, the moving picture and the radio, the former surpasses the latter as an educator. Only in its larger reach can the radio be recognized as having superior advantage. That which is merely said to a pupil may not always convey the idea designed, since language has its limitations as a means of communication, especially when it is used incorrectly and the vocabulary is not large. But let the eye rest on some object related to the truth to be conveyed, and almost immediately the dubious look on the child's face gives way to the smile of comprehension.

a. Objects

There is a difference in using objects for study and for illustration. When Christ placed a child in the center of the group, it was not that the little one might be the subject of a discussion, but a striking illustration of His instruction on humility. As He taught the great truths of the kingdom of heaven on the hillside, it is natural to suppose that He pointed to the "sower that went forth to sow." As His "school" assembled by the Sea of Galilee, perhaps in front of their eyes there were fishermen casting their nets into the sea. When He said, "Behold the fowls of the air," and, "Consider the lilies of the field," language would suggest that these objects were at hand for Him to use as illustrations. The shepherd and his sheep, a common sight in Palestine, must have been used to illustrate as well as inspire the many lessons that He drew from them.

b. Pictures

All classes cannot meet in the country or have access to the living objects that characterized our Lord's instruction. Pictures and photographs may be substituted. A Bible illustrated in colors is most appropriate for boys and girls just beginning to read. What words may fail to convey, the picture is sure to communicate. Aside from the use of Bibles of this character, every teacher should be a collector of pictures, so that from an accumulated supply, suitable ones may be selected for the week's lesson. Just as magazine articles are made doubly attractive by appropriate engravings, so the dullness of a lesson may be relieved by whatever pictures are used for its illustration.

c. Models

Models of the ark, the temple, and Oriental houses will convey truth far more readily and accurately than architectural specifications and detailed descriptions. Even crude blackboard

Illustration 189

drawings and diagrams are invaluable. The larger the number of blackboard or chart outlines used in teaching, the more deeply the mind is impressed. This applies to the older as well as the younger pupils, and there is no age with which a teacher cannot use a blackboard to advantage.

d. Maps

Maps always help a pupil to visualize locations, and should be used constantly, especially in lessons that involve the movements of its characters. Bibles that provide an ample supply of maps are always to be preferred; but in addition, large wall maps, which can be easily consulted, are a valuable means of conveying a correct estimate of situations and distance.

2. Verbal

When an illustration must be presented by means of the ear-gate to gain entrance, it is most important that simple language be used. Because of the limited vocabulary of the child, care should be exercised in the selection of words lest the mind of the pupil be distracted in struggling with the meaning of some unfamiliar word that is being used.

a. Stories

As Spurgeon has already suggested, there is nothing like the introduction of stories to command interest, as well as to relieve dullness of perception.[2] D. L. Moody recognized the possibility of making his messages clear to the masses by fascinating incidents. In his preaching he was unexcelled as a story-teller, and his printed sermons have attracted millions largely because of his ability to recast truth in story form.

(1). Bible

The very best verbal illustrations for the Sunday school teacher are found in the Bible itself, and therefore a complete knowledge of its narrative is essential. As the Bible story conveys the truth as God intended, one need not fear in the

[2] Spurgeon, *op. cit.*, p. 353.

telling lest it should overshadow the lesson it illustrates, since it constitutes a God-given lesson in itself.

(2). *Life*

Next to the Bible stories, the teacher will get his best illustrations from the same place the Master-Teacher found His. While he may not be able to direct the eye, the teacher can please the ear with familiar sights and scenes. Real stories are always the best, and should be told as vividly as possible, although always faithfully portraying the details and not sacrificing the truth. Care must be exercised that in our enthusiasm to paint a vivid picture we do not exaggerate. Stories which contain improbable details lose their power and interest.

b. Comparisons

Making comparisons is one of the easiest and simplest methods of illustration. Because of older pupils' greater knowledge and wider experience, this method can be used more successfully with them. It is not enough to say that sin is a dreadful thing and something to be avoided, but what is it like? The Bible likens sin to that loathsome and dreaded disease of leprosy. You will find it interesting to note how frequently our Lord used comparisons in His instruction. He declared of Himself, "I am the bread of life"; "I am the living water"; "I am the Good Shepherd"; "I am the vine, ye are the branches." He called His disciples "the salt of the earth," "the light of the world."

c. Allusions

An appeal to the intelligence of older pupils may be made by historical, biographical, literary, and scientific allusions. This saves the times necessary to tell a story and fully serves the purpose of illustration in an educated group. Note how frequently the scholarly Paul by similes and metaphors re-

Illustration 191

ferred to nearly every walk of life. Dr. H. T. Kuist has pointed out that from his allusions it can be ascertained that Paul was familiar with law, medicine, architecture, warfare, agriculture, Greek games, seafaring life, and commercial life.[3]

III. VITALITY

What makes an illustration vital? It is just as important to understand the right use of an illustration as to understand the art of questioning. To be vital an illustration must be:

1. Brief

Miss Plummer says: "Illustrations are to be employed as a scaffold is used for a building. No more of it is put up than is actually necessary; and the edifice when completed, is expected to stand by itself." [4] Whenever pupils become more absorbed in the illustration than the lesson itself, the illustration ceases to serve its purpose. When pupils remember the objects that have been exhibited or the story that has been told, and do not recall the instruction, the illustration may be more of a hindrance than a help. Brevity of statement that omits details may be used to adorn the main instruction, so that the illustration may be dismissed from the mind as soon as its object is accomplished.

2. New

Illustrations may be rendered obnoxious by repetition. Old stories oft retold betray poverty or vanity on the part of the teacher, while the pupils lose their interest in the lesson and their esteem for the instructor. When the same illustration is used to impress various truths, there is apt to be confusion instead of clarity in the mind of the pupil. The most effective illustrations are drawn from recent events and daily experi-

---

[3] Howard Tillman Kuist, *The Pedagogy of St. Paul*, p. 102.
[4] Plummer, *The Soul-Winning Teacher*, p. 53.

ences with which the pupils are all familiar. They possess a
freshness that will make their appeal to every wide-awake
boy and girl.

3. Apt

There are illustrations that do not illustrate. If there is only
a faint resemblance, or none at all, between the illustration
and the instruction to be illuminated, nothing is accomplished
by its use.

4. Comprehensible

There is also the danger of using as an illustration some-
thing that is less familiar than the instruction to be clarified.
An oasis means little to one who knows nothing of the desert.
A jungle cannot be visualized by one who lives on a plain.
Even the thought of God as Father may fail in its appeal to
the boy who knows nothing of a father's love in the home.

Illustrations should be on the plane of the learner's experience. If they are too simple they will excite the contempt of
the pupil. If they are too complicated they will not be grasped.
If the teacher knows his pupils—their school attainments,
home life, desires and interests—mistakes will be avoided. It
is hardly necessary to say that an incomprehensible illustration
is far worse than none.

5. Elevating

Illustrations may degrade the truth and debase the hearer
by their poor taste. Illustrations are likely to be bridges leading the thoughts down into the more entertaining and less
hallowed regions from whence they are drawn. A teacher who
makes too frequent use of humorous illustrations may be
popular with his class, but his influence spiritually will be
weakened, for the pupils will learn to think lightly of sacred
things. Illustrations that lack in dignity may seriously weaken
a teacher's best efforts to impress a solemn truth.

Lester B. Mathewson, in his splendid textbook on *The Il-*

Illustration 193

lustration, provides a self-correcting course, covering every phase of its origin and use. In the chapter he devotes to the use of illustrations with boys and girls, he lays down some important principles:

1. Never talk down to boys and girls. They resent any patronizing manner.

2. Everything you say must be within the range of their experience or understanding. One may tell many incidents or facts that are outside of their experience, if they are within the realm of their understanding.

3. The teacher's manner must be friendly and sympathetic with all that concerns them. Children want to know first of all if you understand their life, their ambitions, troubles, problems, perplexities, their ways of looking at things.

4. Be careful about letting them ask questions. If allowed to ask questions indiscriminately, their interrogations will probably be irrelevant or embarrassing to the teacher.

5. Words should be chosen carefully, so they will convey the meaning you desire. Boys and girls sometimes use words with a different meaning which they attach to them other than what adults generally give.

6. In speaking to children, the one prime factor on the human side is your personality, which must be of such nature that it draws children to you and wins attention when you speak.[5]

QUESTIONS

1. How is the illustration related to the law of apperception?
2. Show how illustrations were frequently employed by Old and New Testament writers.
3. What is the danger in too frequent use of illustrations?
4. Name four types of visual illustrations.

[5] Mathewson, *The Illustration in Sermon, Address, Conversation and Teaching,* p. 150.

5. How did our Lord use objects for illustrations?
6. How do models and maps illustrate the lesson material?
7. Contrast visual and verbal illustrations.
8. Why are Bible stories always preferable?
9. What was the threefold purpose of a parable?
10. a. With whom should allusions be used?
    b. Why should they be used?
11. Name five requisites for a vital illustration.
12. When do illustrations not illustrate?

15

Application

THE educational process involves four steps: acquisition, assimilation, appropriation, and application of knowledge. The *acquisition* of knowledge may be likened to the hasty reading of a book. Its contents are not *assimilated* until by further reading we fully understand and remember its information. When certain passages are marked with the thought of future usefulness, we have made an *appropriation* of knowledge. Finally, when in an article or address some quotation is made from its pages, or some truth expressed is reproduced in the life, there is an *application* of knowledge.

The real test of a teacher's work is not what he says to his pupils, but what his pupils say and do as a result of his instruction. Education is not completed in the acquisition, but in the use of knowledge. An educator is one who "leads out," and this leading-out process results in the application of truth. In the last analysis, the pupil is not merely to learn facts, but to apply them.

The teacher cannot be constantly with his pupils. There are many influences that tend to counteract his instruction. This is all the more reason that our teaching should be vitally related to the lives of our pupils; and if it is to be so related, the teacher must know as much as possible about their problems. The teacher may also seek to keep parents informed as to the work the Sunday school is trying to do, and to enlist their cooperation in providing opportunities for real application of the Sunday school lesson.

As we have already seen, the supreme purpose of the Christian teacher is to shape the immortal destiny of a soul according to the Word of God. The imparting of biblical knowledge is a comparatively simple matter. The development of Christian character is far more difficult. Yet the teacher has not done all that is required unless there is evidence of a response in the *life* of the pupil. When the practice of righteousness can be observed in the life of a pupil, the teacher may then be assured that he has sufficiently impressed biblical truths in his instruction so that they are being expressed in action. We cannot, of course, separate character and Christian living. Character develops through living, and in turn expresses itself in living. The Christian life is the outward expression of the Christ-formed character within.

We have already learned in child study that the basis of character is habit. Habit is often called "second nature." When habits are fixed and become our master, we may well say with Wellington, "Habit is ten times nature." All application of truth should first address itself to the establishment of habits that will prove a blessing throughout life. Among the habits aimed at by the Christian teacher are Bible study, prayer, reverence, worship, obedience, and unselfishness. These should be in the teacher's thoughts in the preparation of the lesson, as well as in the teaching of it.

We have also previously learned that character is strengthened by expression. Character does not grow through dreaming or wishing or talking. Character grows through doing. The habit of doing nothing, like the habit of doing wrong, is bad. Instruction and inspiration that do not find expression in action, harden our sensitive natures, and make us less ready to respond on another occasion. It is obvious that expressional activities must constitute a large part of our teaching program if positive, active Christian character is to be developed in our pupils.

One cannot study the teaching methods of our Lord without being impressed with the emphasis which He laid on the application of His instruction. After the Sermon on the Mount He said, "Whosoever heareth these sayings of mine, and *doeth* them, I will liken him unto a wise man, which built his house upon a rock" (Matt. 7:24). "Not every one that saith unto me, Lord, Lord, shall enter into the kingdom of heaven; but he that *doeth* the will of my Father which is in heaven" (Matt. 7:21). When He declared, "By their fruits ye shall know them" (Matt. 7:20), did He not mean that the quality and value of a man's religion will be manifest by deeds and actions? Christ's class was in itself a life-sharing project. When they enrolled for His instruction they discovered that He would teach them in terms of activity. They did not learn in a formal schoolroom, but by sharing His work with Him. Later, when they had learned to live as He lived, and adopted His spiritual attitudes toward God and their fellow men, He sent them out to complete their training by some practical experience.

In the same way the Christian teacher can help his pupils to form Christian habits of thought and action. They can be taught to pray, not so much by defining or describing prayer as by entering actively into the class prayer period. They can be taught to study the Bible, not so much by telling them of its excellencies as by providing a lesson which will in its preparation and recitation require the pupils to *use* the Bible. They can best be taught reverence, obedience, unselfishness by the *practice* of these virtues.

In making the application, there are three important considerations.

I. THE APPLICATION OF THE WORD OF GOD

The shaping of the eternal destiny of a soul must be in accordance with the Bible and not apart from it. Only the Word of God provides the principles for Christian living, and to attempt to build character independent of its instruction is useless. Modern educators, in their zeal for the application of truth, have lost sight of its acquisition. In focusing their attention on the experiences of the pupil, they have intimated that the contents of a book written centuries ago are not suited for modern application. But the Bible is the changeless book for the changing age, and its contents will always be profitable for instruction. To expect the pupil to start with nothing and build up a Christian or religious faith solely from his everyday experiences is tantamount to attempting to reach port on an ocean voyage without chart, compass, or pilot. The Bible is full of life experiences. It is absurd to imagine that a teacher cannot enter into a child's life unless the subject of his instruction is some topic of current events. That Bible school lessons should center on sports, social activities, and pupils' experiences, to develop some moral truths in their lives, is lamentable. It is time that modern educators realized that it is possible to teach the Bible and still aim that teaching directly at the greatest life needs of our pupils. Bible-centered and life-centered lessons are not the impossibility that so many present-day leaders in religious education imagine. The determination of these educators to apply Bible truth before a knowledge of it is acquired would indicate that they have by-passed the supreme authority of the Bible.

Although our Lord laid great stress on application in His religious program, He always based it on the Word of God. When He went into the synagogue at Nazareth, He read and expounded the first two verses of Isaiah 61. And His exposition was an up-to-date application. He said that the words of this ancient prophet were fulfilled that *very day*. Again, after His resurrection, He met the disappointed disciples on the road to Emmaus, and, as a master-teacher, drew out from them in conversation the reason for their perplexity. And how did He meet this situation in real life—how did He comfort these sorrowful disciples? Why, "he expounded unto them in all the scriptures the things concerning himself" (Luke 24:27). Certainly this was Bible teaching if there ever was such teaching. But it was applied instruction. It was aimed at the greatest need those two disciples felt at that hour. As David R. Piper has pointed out:

> "We must put equal emphasis on two facts which are not contradictory but correlative in Jesus' method. He taught Scripture directly by the expository method and used the Scripture as authority, and yet He taught for the specific purpose of applying the meaning of Scripture to some real life question, problem, or need of those whom He addressed." [1]

II. THE APPLICATION TO THE TEACHER

No teacher can successfully make application of truth to others until he has first applied it to his own life. Dr. J. McConaughey says: "If our pupils are to learn of Christ through us, we must be sure that we really know Him ourselves—that we have been saved from sin by His death on the Cross, and are kept from falling into sin by the help which He daily gives us." Boys and girls must constantly see exemplified in their teacher the truths he seeks to apply to their lives.

Our Lord's supreme work of teaching was accomplished by His daily demonstration of the truths that He taught. He taught humility when He placed a child in the midst of the wrangling disciples. But far more impressive than that object

[1] Piper, *How Would Jesus Teach?* p. 59.

lesson was the memorable occasion when He personified meekness by girding Himself and washing the disciples' feet (John 13:14, 15). He taught the lesson of forgiveness on more than one occasion (Matt. 6:15; 18:21, 22), but it was His look of forgiveness on Peter, after he had denied his Lord three times, that led the impetuous disciple to hurry out and weep bitterly (Luke 22:61, 62). Perhaps our Lord's supreme exhibition of forgiveness, when on the cross He prayed, "Father, forgive them, for they know not what they do," led the hardened centurion to acknowledge that Jesus was a righteous man (Luke 23:34, 47). How did Christ come to teach His disciples how to pray? He had spoken on this subject previously more than once, but the disciples did not seem impressed. On this occasion, however, we read, "And it came to pass, that, *as he was praying* in a certain place, when he ceased, one of his disciples said unto him, Lord, teach us to pray, as John also taught his disciples" (Luke 11:1).

More than one young man has testified that while he had forgotten the instruction of his mother, he never could eradicate from his mind the picture of her kneeling in prayer in his behalf. The teacher who exemplifies his instruction in daily living will make an indelible impression on the hearts and minds of his pupils. No lesson will really be a helpful lesson to the class if it has not been a helpful lesson to the teacher. Its application must be backward toward the teacher before it will go forward toward the class. What has this lesson taught me? is a good question for the teacher to ask. Am I better qualified for my work after studying this lesson than I was before? Am I an exemplification of the truth I am trying to give the scholars? Marion Lawrance says, "This is the crucial part of a teacher's preparation, for after all, the teacher's life is the life of his teaching."

III. APPLICATION TO THE PUPIL

The application of the lesson is closely related to the aim of the teacher, which has already been discussed (Chapter 6); but it will now be in order to give a fuller consideration to this phase of the subject.

In the preparation of the lesson the teacher should plan for the particular needs of his pupils. Every member of the class has specific needs, but application of the instruction can be included under four general heads:

1. Salvation

It is of first importance that every pupil be reminded of his personal responsibility for a decision for Christ. In a class where there are unconverted pupils, all instruction should have for its goal the personal acceptance of Jesus Christ as Saviour and Lord. There is no more essential application of truth than that which leads to the cross. Before the pupil's conversion, the teacher should teach and train in habits that will help the pupil to become a Christian. Among such habits are attendance at church services, Bible study, reverence for God's house and His day.

2. Spirituality

After the pupil's conversion, the teacher should use his opportunity to train in habits that will develop spirituality. As the Sunday school is chiefly a teaching service, the principal habit that should result from attendance is that of Bible study.

The departmental program, however, will afford an opportunity to train in worship. Classes may be selected in advance and prepared to plan and lead these worship periods. This preparation should involve a study of the elements of true worship, a searching of the Scripture for the acts involved in worship, and a study of the worship program of the local church to see how the pastor plans a worship service for his congregation. It will also lead to the reading of prayers, hymns, and devotional books, as well as other books or periodicals which will help the class to understand and appreciate the experience of worship.

Especially should the pupils be encouraged to develop skill in singing religious music and to get enjoyment from it. Almost every child can sing, and all children respond to the appeal of music adapted to their understanding.

The prayer life of the pupil must also be given attention if he is to "grow in grace and in the knowledge of our Lord and Saviour, Jesus Christ." Time taken from the class period for a prayer meeting is not wasted, especially if every pupil can be encouraged to participate. Public attention to prayer will prove a reminder if not an encouragement to fidelity in private devotions.

3. Stewardship

The development of the spiritual life of the pupil includes the obligation of bringing him to see his personal responsibility not only for his use of time, but also for the practice of stewardship, which includes a recognition of his use of his possessions. Pupils should be led early in life into giving money for missionary purposes, and as far as possible it should be money which they have earned. For a child to be given money for an offering does not train him in stewardship. It is the pupil's real sharing of *his* possessions that leaves the impression and teaches the lesson. One of the great truths that the Sunday school needs to learn is that we are "raising" children and not money, and only as the spirit of sacrifice and of sharing enters into the child's offering is there any real gain accomplished.

"Not what we give, but what we share,
  For the gift without the giver is bare;
  He who gives himself with his gifts feeds three,
  Himself, his hungering neighbor, and Me."

The purpose of giving in the Sunday school is to train a generation of liberal, systematic, cheerful givers. The pupils, then, must know to what they give and why they give, and they must give because they want to give.

4. Service

The teaching material should be applied in order to bring the pupil to see his personal responsibility not only for his time and possessions, but for his talents as well. The wise teacher will keep his eyes open for every possible opportunity to find something worth while for his pupils to do. He will endeavor to make his instruction a laboratory course in religion, finding in human needs the opportunities for real service.

a. Home

There is no more important place for service than the home. Children need to see their responsibility for its greatest happiness. They should be encouraged to share in the care of the home and not to shirk their share of its tasks. They should have a definite part in the hospitality which the home extends to its friends and neighbors, and take pride in demonstrating its attractiveness to others.

b. Church

Next to the home, the pupil needs to be impressed with his responsibility to the church of which he is a member. This calls not only for fidelity to its services and systematic, proportionate contributions to its support, but for an active participation in its work. Younger pupils who are not church members can be enlisted as recruiting officers to secure new members for the Sunday school, or to look up those who attend irregularly or have dropped out entirely. Others can be enlisted for messenger service, for in a wide-awake Sunday school there will be articles to be gathered and distributed, and many things which children can do as well as their elders. Service can also be rendered in the class or the school in the distribution of supplies, or decoration of the rooms for special occasions. Older pupils can help in taking a census, which will be used to build up the Sunday school enrollment.

c. Community

In addition to service in the local Sunday school and church, opportunities for it will be found in the community. The successful enlistment of the Boy Scouts and the Girl Scouts in many valuable forms of community enterprises contains a valuable suggestion for the Sunday school. The Boy or Girl Scout takes great pride in doing acts of kindness without personal reward, and the Sunday school can command the same spirit if the proper appeal is made.

d. World

From the community, the program should extend to the world, for there are things to be done for God's children in other lands. Missionary boxes and gifts of money can be the expression of genuine and intelligent interest in the lives of those to whom they go. Pupils must be brought to see their responsibility for the evangelizing of the entire world.

QUESTIONS

1. What are the four steps of the educational process?
2. What does the application of knowledge have to do with the establishment of character?
3. How did our Lord teach in terms of activity?
4. How can the Christian teacher help his pupils form right habits?

5. Why must all applications be based on Bible teaching?
6. Show how our Lord was always careful to observe this important principle.
7. Why must the teacher first apply Bible truth to his own life?
8. Illustrate how our Lord demonstrated this principle.
9. For what four general needs of the pupils should the teacher plan his application?
10. In making applications, why should the salvation and spiritual life of the pupils always be given first consideration?
11. a. Make two suggestions for the pupil's practice of worship.
    b. Make one suggestion for the practice of stewardship.
12. In what four fields of service may pupils be encouraged to apply their instruction?

Part V: *The Teaching*

16

Laws

THE success of any teacher is in a large degree dependent upon his enthusiasm for his task, his love for his pupils, and his thoroughness in preparation. All of these characteristics can be cultivated. In the teaching of the lesson, it will be found that inspiration in presentation is largely the result of perspiration in preparation. Success in teaching can be assured to all who are willing to be guided and corrected by the recognized principles of pedagogy.

But does not that conflict with the work of the Holy Spirit? Ought not every teacher who is living the surrendered life be guided and directed by the Holy Spirit? Is not the Holy Spirit dishonored by the teacher who seeks to be guided by the laws of pedagogy? Not at all. One does not dishonor the Holy Spirit in complying with the laws of gravitation. One does not dishonor the Holy Spirit in becoming acquainted with the laws which govern the working of the human mind. No one was more fully led by the Holy Spirit than our Lord Jesus Christ and yet no one more consistently observed the laws of pedagogy. It is true that He did not write a text on the technique of teaching, and as far as we know none was in existence in His day. It is obvious however, that He and the teachers of His day were masters in the art and practice of teaching.

[1] The seven laws of teaching (old, but reliable) by John Milton Gregory not only embody the principles of pedagogy employed by our Lord, but they also constitute excellent rules for the evaluation of the work of a teacher.

I. THE LAW OF THE TEACHER

Dr. Gregory says: "Good character and rare moral qualities are desirable in an instructor of the young; if not in his actual work, at least to prevent harm from his example. But if, one by one, we dismiss from our catalogue of needful qualifications for the work of teaching those not absolutely indispensable, we shall find ourselves obliged to retain at last, as necessary to the very notion of teaching, a knowledge of the subject matter to be taught." The first and foremost law, then, is: *The teacher must know that which he would teach.* In secular education a knowledge of the subject constitutes the very heart of teaching. We dare not permit the inference that religious instruction is of so much less importance that the mastery of the Bible is not essential. Knowledge is the material with which the teacher works, and therefore it must be complete. Imperfect knowledge is reflected in imperfect teaching. A man cannot teach effectively what he does not know. A lack of knowledge of that which is to be taught cripples and cramps the entire process of instruction more than anything else.

Miss Plummer says: "In our study of the Scripture we should strive to be thorough. We should dig deep; the best jewels are mined far below the surface. Accuracy is always in demand. The bookkeeper's columns must be correct to a cent. The carpenter's joints must fit exactly, otherwise his work is botched. Each lesson thoroughly mastered gives added power for the next, but every lesson skimmed over only weak-

[1] Gregory, *The Seven Laws of Teaching*, pp. 3, 4.

ens us for that which awaits us in the future. The difference between success and failure, between feebleness and power, is that of invincible, persistent determination on the one hand, and lack of energy and a yielding before difficulties on the other." [2]

The teacher should know *more* than he can teach. It is not sufficient to know just enough to fill in the time. There must be earnest study and close investigation in order to have a complete grasp of the lesson. Unlike the preacher, the teacher needs to be sufficiently well informed on the subject to answer any question his pupils may ask. More than that, instead of a feeling of incompetence and subservience to his preparation, the teacher who is a master of his subject can watch the effect of his efforts on the class and direct with ease the trend of their thought and participation.

II. THE LAW OF THE PUPIL

Long before Spurgeon became London's famous preacher, he had acquired a reputation as a children's worker. In his instructions to teachers he says: "Get the children's attention. If they do not hearken, you may talk, but you will speak to no purpose whatever. If they do not listen, you go through your labors as an unmeaning drudgery to yourselves and your scholars, too. You can do nothing without securing their attention." This counsel is in keeping with the second law of padagogy—*The pupil must attend with interest to the lesson to be learned.*

Dr. McKinney says: "In looking forward to meeting his class on Sunday, the teacher who is interesting to his pupils, prayerfully prepares for accomplishing three things for his class. His first endeavor is to gain their attention. He next puts forth every effort to retain that attention throughout the study

[2] Plummer, *The Soul Winning Teacher,* p. 44.

period. But his most difficult work is to turn that attention into interest." [3]

It is easy to gain and hold the attention of an interested pupil. A peremptory command or a sleight-of-hand performance may briefly divert attention, but real interest alone will sustain it. As Dr. Goodrich C. White suggests: "We must find a way to give boys and girls things to do that seem worth while to us and at the same time will seem so worth while to them that they will crowd other things out of mind." [4]

III. THE LAW OF THE LANGUAGE

We have discovered the teacher with his important equipment of knowledge on the one hand, and the pupil with his requisite of interested attention on the other. The next step is to set up a successful medium of communication between them. This law may be stated thus: *The language used in instruction must be common to teacher and pupil.*

The teacher may have a much larger vocabulary than the pupil, but it must be remembered that only insofar as the teacher limits himself to the language of the pupil will his instruction be comprehended. The language employed must of necessity differ for every department, if not for every age in the Sunday school. To this end Dr. Gregory suggests that the teacher:

1. Study constantly and carefully the language of the pupils.

2. Express himself as far as possible in their language.

3. Use the simplest and fewest words that will express his meaning.

4. Use short sentences of the simplest construction.

[3] McKinney, *Practical Pedagogy in the Sunday School,* p. 90.
[4] White, *Teaching in the Sunday School,* p. 22.

5. Explain the meaning of new words by illustrations.

6. Test frequently the pupils' understanding of the words he uses.

IV. THE LAW OF THE LESSON

This law, which deals directly with the lesson or truth to be taught, is fundamental to all pedagogy. It may be stated thus: *The truth to be taught must be learned through truth already known.*

All teaching must begin at some known point of the lesson. If the subject is entirely new, then a known point must be sought so that by comparison with something known and familiar there may be understanding. This law of association or contact is basic for all mental development. The new can be understood only in terms of the old.

Our Lord was a master of the law of apperception. His hearers were all familiar with the Old Testament. For this reason He constantly built new truths on these well-known facts. His crucifixion on the cross was to be similar to the lifting up of the brazen serpent in the wilderness. His burial and resurrection were likened to the experiences through which Jonah had passed. The times of His return would be like the days of Noah and the days of Lot. He described things which were to come in terms of things that had already happened.

To observe the law of apperception the teacher should:

1. Make contact with former lessons

What has previously been studied lies in the realm of the known. If the teacher has taught former lessons this will be familiar ground to both instructor and pupils. Every review, in one sense, is a demonstration of the law of apperception, and those who are faithful in their attention to reviews best observe this principle.

2. Proceed by graded steps

An athlete does not set his mark at an unattained height and then attempt to jump it. He starts at a lower level which he knows from previous experience can be successfully cleared, and then advances inch by inch until a new record is established. In the same way the pupil must fully grasp each step before the next is taken. Each new idea mastered becomes a part of the pupil's knowledge and serves as a starting place for a fresh advance. Like a series of lamps on a highway, the new idea adds its own light to what precedes it and throws the increased illumination forward for the next discovery.

3. Illuminate by illustration

The illustration is nothing more than a retreat to familiar ground. When the advance is more rapid than the mind can follow, temporary retirement to known scenes permits the lagging understanding to catch up.

D. L. Moody recognized the possibilities of making his messages clear to the masses by frequently interjecting illustrations. Figures of speech such as similes, metaphors, and allegories, have sprung out of the need for relating new truth to old and familiar scenes and experiences.

V. THE LAW OF THE TEACHING PROCESS

The teacher is sometimes compared to a chauffeur who starts and guides his car. The pupil is carefully fed with such short and simple portions of the Bible as he can assimilate and apply. But to the teaching material it is found necessary to apply the spark of interest to ignite the fuel and produce action. Once the teacher has thoroughly aroused and fully interested the pupil, all that remains is to take his seat and guide and direct the latter's activities. In a word, the real work of the teacher is to stimulate and direct thought, or as stated in the fifth law: *Excite and direct the self-activities of the pupil, and as a rule tell him nothing that he can learn for himself.*

If the pupil does not think for himself there are no results in teaching. In fact, the great aim of the teacher is to make the pupil a discoverer of truth. The learning process actually begins when the pupil becomes an independent investigator. It is well to recognize that knowledge can be obtained without a teacher, and that we have successful self-made men who have never had the privilege of attending schools of higher learning. What then is the use of schools and the necessity of a teacher? The teacher is needed to provide the most favorable conditions for self-learning. True teaching is not so much imparting knowledge, as stimulating the pupil to acquire it for himself.

How can thought be stimulated? Three suggestions are given for the teacher:

1. **Provide thought-material**

The action of the mind is limited practically to the field of its acquired knowledge. The pupil who knows nothing cannot think, for he has nothing to think about. In order to compare, criticize, judge, and reason, the mind must necessarily work on the material in its possession. For that reason it is necessary first to store the pupil's mind with the facts which will serve as the basis of his thought. Modern education which seeks to draw out knowledge from a child's experience without first implanting it, is attempting to pump out information from a vacuum. True, education is a drawing-out process; but no one has been able to tell how any teacher can draw out knowledge that has not previously been implanted.

2. **Ask questions**

The most important stimulus used by nature to stir the mind is the ceaseless questions the world and the universe are always addressing to man. The object or event that excites no question will provoke no thought. Questioning is not, there-fore, merely one of the devices of teaching. It is really the whole of teaching. It is the exciting of self-activity on the part of the pupil to the discovery of truth. To ask a question is to set the wheels of the pupil's mind working.

3. Provoke questions

Even more important than asking questions is arousing the spirit of inquiry. In fact, the educational process begins only when pupils ask questions. The eternal questions of child-hood are echoed in the mature mind that grapples with the problems of the universe. The falling apple had the question of gravitation in it for the inquiring mind of Newton, and the boiling teakettle propounded to Watt the problem of a steam engine. The pupil's question is not only an index to his mind, but an index to himself. His question is a manifesta-tion of self-realization and self-seeking. By encouraging the pupil to ask questions, the teacher stimulates a natural quest for knowledge, as well as a natural desire for expression.

VI. THE LAW OF THE LEARNING PROCESS

It has been seen that the teacher's work consists largely in arousing and guiding the self-activities of the pupils. Atten-tion must now be given to the pupil's response to the teacher's efforts. The learning process involves more than manifesting interest and giving attention. There is a clear and distinct act or process which the pupil must perform. This act or process is to form in his own mind, by the use of his own powers, a true concept of the facts or principles of the lesson. This law of the learning process may be stated thus: *The pupil must reproduce in his own mind the truth to be learned, then express it in his own words.*

Contrary to general opinion, the work of education is much

more the work of the pupil than the teacher. While we can learn rapidly from others, and original discovery is a slow, laborious process, yet no true learning is wholly a repetition of the thoughts of others. The discoverer borrows largely of facts known to others, to which he adds that which he learns from his own experience. The teacher conforms to this law insofar as he brings the pupil to be an independent investigator.

There are three distinct stages of learning, each one carrying the pupil farther toward the mastery of his lesson.

1. Reproduction

It is possible to reproduce the exact words of the lesson by committing it to memory. This is all that is attempted by many pupils, or required by teachers who have little conception of how much is involved in the learning process. If the pupil does not understand what he has memorized, apart from the mental discipline, he cannot be said to *possess* the lesson. A man may purchase a book and place it in his library, and yet make no use of it whatever.

2. Interpretation

There is a decided advance in the learning process when the pupil is able to give more than the actual words or facts that he has learned. When he can express his own opinion on these facts it is evidence not only that he understands what he has been taught, but that he has learned to deal with his own thoughts as well as the thoughts of others. Failure to insist on original thinking by the pupils is one of the most common faults of teachers. In questioning, instead of so frequently using the word "what" which calls for only factual answers, a good teacher will employ the word "why," until the pupil is brought to feel that he is expected to have an opinion in the matter.

3. Application

Education is not the acquisition but the use of knowledge, and no lesson is fully learned until some effort has been made to apply it to everyday life. The pupil who finds a use for what he has learned in his lesson becomes doubly interested. What was idle knowledge, then becomes practical wisdom. Knowledge is power only when it is conquered, harnessed, and set to work. While to express an opinion exercises only the mind, to apply knowledge, affects the will and involves the very life of the pupil. Practical applications are persistently neglected. Many a Sunday school pupil is "always learning, but never able to come to a knowledge of the truth" because there has been no personal application of the lesson to his own life.

VII. THE LAW OF REVIEW AND APPLICATION

Business sessions are opened with the reading of the minutes of the last meeting, and closed with the minutes of that day's proceedings. There is a review of what transpired both at the beginning and end of the meeting. The first is necessary to establish a closer relationship with former sessions, and the second, to carry over the day's proceedings to the next assembly. We have already noted the importance of making contact with former lessons at the beginning of the session. It is equally essential that the outstanding truths of the day's instruction be carried over to the next lesson, and that they be vitalized in the lives of the pupils. The law of review and application may be expressed as follows: *The completion, test, and confirmation of the work of teaching must be made by review and application.*

There are three aims in the review, or recapitulation, of the lesson:

1. To perfect knowledge

A review is more than a repetition. A new lesson or fresh topic never reveals all of itself at first. It often distracts the attention, and its novelty may dazzle the mind. When you look at a picture for the first time you will miss many of its details. These will be revealed only as you return to examine it more closely. A second reading of a book will bring out facts that were entirely missed at the first perusal. There is no book like the Bible for rereading to find new material. Even a review of familiar passages never fails to reveal new light or disclose new lessons.

2. To confirm knowledge

Memory depends on the association of ideas. Each review familiarizes and strengthens these ideas through an added association. A person may be introduced to a group of people and not be sure of all their names, but when another stranger is presented a few minutes later, his knowledge will be confirmed and his memory strengthened. The lesson that is studied but once is likely learned only to be forgotten, but that which is repeatedly reviewed, becomes a part of our equipment of knowledge. Not that which a pupil has once learned and recited, but that which he permanently remembers and uses, is the correct measure of his achievement.

3. To apply knowledge

Frequently, practice makes a skilled artist, and frequent and thorough reviews render knowledge ready and useful. The Scripture texts which most influence us are those which have become familiar by use and which arise in our minds as occasion demands. The plastic power of truth to shape conduct and mold character belongs only to the truths which have become familiar by repetition. If we would have any great truth sustain and control us, we must return to it until it becomes habitually fixed in our lives. The "line upon line and precept upon precept" rule of the Bible is a recognition of this truth.

In conclusion, the review is not an added excellence in teaching, but one of the essential conditions of all true teaching. Not to review is to leave the work half done.

QUESTIONS

1. Show that the work of the Holy Spirit is not dishonored by an acquaintance and compliance with the laws of pedagogy.
2. What is the law of the teacher?
3. Why must the teacher know more than he can teach?
4. What is the law of the pupil?
5. Suggest four ways in which the law of the language can be observed.
6. Upon what four things will interest depend?
7. Define the law of the language, and name four ways in which the teacher can observe this law.
8. State three ways in which the law of the lesson can be observed.
9. What is the law of the teaching process?
10. Suggest three ways in which thought can be stimulated.
11. Define the law of the learning process, and state the three distinct stages of learning.
12. What are the three aims of the law of review and application?

17

Methods

IN A PREVIOUS lesson it was pointed out that the supreme purpose of the Christian teacher is to shape the immortal destiny of a soul according to the Word of God. This must be kept in mind as we consider the general mode of procedure to be followed in teaching, as well as the specific methods which may be employed in the development of the lesson.

I. MODE OF PROCEDURE

There are two historic lines of reasoning recognized in the process of thinking, the *deductive* and the *inductive*. In deductive logic, reasoning is from general truth to particular truth, in which no more is inferred in the conclusion than is implicitly contained in the premise. Inductive logic, on the other hand, reaches a general conclusion by reasoning from a number of particular propositions. In religious teaching today, these historic plans of procedure are represented by the expository and the experience modes.

1. Expository mode

The plan of this procedure is to take the statements of Scripture as general truths and deduct from them, verse by verse, particular lessons. These applications may be made one by one as the Scripture is unfolded, or gathered at the end of the study and driven home to the heart of the scholar. This mode answers the question, What does the Bible say? It sets forth the thought of the writer of Scripture as he intended it, and makes the impression on the mind of the scholar which the writer himself desired to convey. This is an exact, faithful, reverential, and effective mode of teaching the Word of God.

Excellent as it is, this plan is not without limitations. Three difficulties are encountered.

a. Lack of time

One cannot explain the historical background, the terms and expressions, and the content even of a single verse, without consuming a larger proportion of time than the only too brief hour the Sunday school session allows. In consequence, very little ground can be covered in the period usually allotted to teaching the class.

b. Lack of interest

Interest of necessity starts from the viewpoint of the pupil, and the untrained teacher will experience difficulty in making a point of contact between the thoughts of modern children and the writings of ancient times. His difficulties in awakening interest are further increased by the unfamiliar language of Scripture and the spiritual significance of its content.

c. Lack of application

While "all scripture is profitable for doctrine, for reproof, for correction, for instruction in righteousness," few pupils, especially children, have had sufficient experience in Christian living to appreciate the application of all Bible truth. Expository teaching presupposes some understanding and experimental knowledge of Scripture.

2. Experience mode

The experience mode is the favorite plan of modern educators, and is just the reverse of the expository mode. It proceeds from the experience of the pupil, or some application that has been made, to find by inductive thinking the great underlying truth of Scripture. A preacher exemplifies this plan of procedure when he chooses for his sermon a topic, rather than a text, that fits into the language and experience of his hearers, and from that point leads his audience to discover some basic Bible truth. He does not experience difficulty in arousing interest, nor does he lose time in unfolding the meaning of unrelated verses, or explaining the obscure words or phrases. Moreover, application is assured, since that is the point from which the beginning is made.

This mode likewise has its limitations. It is more likely to wander at random over Scripture and make its study a secondary aim. The teacher naturally is more concerned about what the Bible teaches than about what it says, so that this mode is really one of interpretation rather than instruction. It is liable to create human applications and then seek to substantiate them from Scripture truth. It tends to center the study in human experience rather than in the Word of God, and by a forced interpretation of a biblical passage ignore its relationship to what precedes and follows. It often reveals a profound ignorance of the Bible as a whole in its efforts to associate an unnatural application.

Since it is the supreme purpose of the Christian teacher to shape the immortal destiny of the soul *according to the Word of God,* it is most important that a mode of procedure be followed that will *impart* that content of Scripture before attempting to *apply* it. The distinguishing fact of biblical religion is the approach of God to man, and therefore, it is an implanting rather than a developing. Revelation presupposes capacity for reception, but it also presupposes ignorance. "All scripture is profitable for instruction" suggests that the content of Scripture must first be implanted before it is serviceable and applicable, or rather, before "the man of God may be perfect, throughly furnished unto all good works" (II Tim. 3:16). The superiority of the expository mode for this purpose is obvious. Speaking in its favor, Dr. Schmauk says: [1]

"It is the one way to make pupils acquainted with Scripture. It sets up the Scripture itself as the only rule of faith and life. When a section or chapter of the Bible has been studied under this expository plan, the pupil becomes possessed of the real and full meaning of the Scripture, and accepts the Word of God as the writer understood it when he wrote it." If the Bible speaks with the authority of the Word of God, it cannot be taught any other way.

Granted then that the expository mode should be chosen as the mode of procedure, how may its difficulties be overcome? In the same way that mathematics may be attractively presented and successfully taught to any pupil. Interest can be aroused not only by a knowledge of the child, but also by a comprehensive, graded development of the subject, while application can be assured by a program of correlated expressional activities. Time will be required, it is true, but why should not children devote as much time to the study of the Bible as to the study of mathematics?

However, aside from the adoption of a correct mode of procedure, success in teaching will rest largely on the methods selected for the development of the instruction.

II. METHODS OF DEVELOPMENT

All pupils cannot be taught by the same method. All lessons cannot be equally well presented by the same method. A good teacher will be familiar with all methods. Five are suggested:

1. Story-telling

The first great gift, especially in teaching little children, is the ability to tell a story. It is the favorite method in the

[1] Theodore E. Schmauk, *How to Teach in Sunday School*, p. 110.

Beginners and Primary departments, and can be used to advantage even with Juniors. As a large portion of the Bible is narrative, it may be readily seen how excellently the reproduction of Scripture content in story form fits into the expository mode of procedure. Jesus, Master-Teacher, was a good story-teller. His recorded stories have never been surpassed as models of graphic character painting by means of action and spoken word. What constitutes a good story? Dr. Goodrich C. White says that it must be:

a. Interesting

Probably there is no other teaching method by which attention can be more easily gained and held. This is because of the interest aroused at the outset. The Bible tells a thrilling, fascinating story, so that any part of its narrative can be made interesting.

b. Dramatic

Story-telling, because the eye as well as the ear is enlisted, is sometimes called the dramatic method. It presents a moving drama linked together by verbs of action. All the great Bible stories possess conflict, plot, suspense—characteristics that make a dramatic story. Verbs will abound, but adjectives will be used sparingly. Sentences will be short. Language will be simple. By look, gesture, and facial expression the teacher himself will act and will gain admittance through the eye-gate when ears may be dull of hearing.

c. Full of action

Action is essential. And "full of action" does not mean "full of words." Often action is intensified by the restriction of words. The stories Jesus told are of achievement. He did not use a single word to describe the *Good* Samaritan, but his character was clearly pictured by his deeds.

d. True to life

The impossible never appeals like that which is in the realm of achievement for every boy and girl. A fairy tale does not leave the pupil any hope of realization. The true story will command the larger interest. It is the element of truth that characterizes Bible stories and makes them superior to all others. [2]

In addition to Dr. White's suggestions, it may be said that stories should have few characters if the boys and girls are not to be confused. Moreover, stories should have direct discourse to permit a simple presentation. The characters should talk instead of the teacher's attempting to report what they are saying. Children like to see life, even in inanimate things.

2. Recitation

While the story is excellent to gain and to hold attention, it has its disadvantages. A pupil fed too richly with stories will not grow mentally. His intellectual development requires that he be more than a listener. It is necessary that the mental process of listening give way to more active participation. The pupil must do some work. The process of absorption must give way before the more active process as assimilation and reproduction. Education is in reality a drawing-out process, and for this reason the recitation method should be used. It is employed most effectively in the Primary and Junior departments. Dr. Schmauk points out some of its advantages:

(1) It gets the pupil to work on his own initiative. He prepares the lesson, and comes to the recitation with some familiarity, if not mastery, of the subject.

(2) If the assignment is memory work, the subject matter will be definitely marked off and limited in the mind of teacher and scholar. It provides an opportunity to drill and to test the memory.

(3) The pupil is more apt to take away a few definite and well-fixed facts and truths.

[2] White, *Teaching in the Sunday School*, p. 45.

(4) The teacher, through his questions and the replies he receives, will gain a better insight into the pupil's mind.

(5) It provides the teacher an opportunity to train his pupils to use language correctly, naturally, and fluently.

(6) It enables the teacher to discover the pupil who is intellectually lazy, and to give him more frequent occasions to express himself.[3]

No recitation will be successful if conducted merely as a piece of routine. To insist that the pupil merely recite in the language of the textbook will dull his originality and fail to call forth any activity except that of memory.

3. Discussion

While the recitation brings the pupil into action by requiring his reproduction of the lesson, this method has its limitations in that the pupil merely transmits knowledge without making it his own. He may acquire knowledge without appropriating it. For this reason the discussion method is employed to advantage, especially in adolescent and adult classes. Under this type, there is a continuous development or gradual construction of the lesson. In stimulating the spirit of inquiry and in arousing personal interest, it has no superior. No other method is as well adapted for securing individual expression or application of the lesson.

One of the greatest difficulties, next to starting a discussion and keeping it going, is to direct it along the line of the lesson. Some member of the class may manifest major interest in a minor item and much time may be lost before the class can be brought back to the main track. These side departures make it extremely difficult to complete the lesson in the given time. Another disadvantage lies in the overtalkative pupil's monopolizing the time, thus giving no opportunity to the reticent, retiring person who needs experience in expression.

[3] Schmauk, *op. cit.*, p. 72.

But with all of its difficulties, this group discussion or con-ference method, when properly managed, remains the most nearly ideal of all teaching methods. Not only does it en-courage expressional activity on the part of the pupils, but it forces them to form their own judgments rather than passively to accept or unthinkingly to reject those presented by the teacher. It hardly need be added that a profitable discussion will depend in no small degree on what previous preparation has been made both by the teacher and by the class.

If the members of a class take this method seriously, each will feel a sense of responsibility for the conduct of the ses-sion. Every member will take his turn at "carrying the ball." To the extent that each person participates to the limit of his ability, attention and interest will be sustained.

4. Research

We have explained that in the technique of teaching the great aim is to make the pupil an independent investigator. There is no better method for this than that of research. Here the teacher assigns to each pupil a part of the lesson to in-vestigate. During the lesson period each member of the class presents his part, which is commented upon, given an evalua-tion, and organized by the teacher into the combined result of the work for that day. This method can be used effectively in adolescent and adult classes, provided books and materials are available for research, and the class is sufficiently small to give each member an opportunity to report his findings.

One of the principal difficulties is to maintain the interest of the rest of the class while one of the members is presenting his assignment. For that reason it is recommended that:

a. Reports be brief

If possible, every member of the class should participate, and the time should be proportionately divided among them, with ample time for the teacher to sum up the findings. Full attendance of the class is an important factor.

b. Reports be correlated

Interest can be sustained when the parts so well fit into each other that curiosity will be aroused as to the outcome of the completed preparation. The teacher can accomplish this by making suitable assignments and distributing them to the best advantage.

5. Lecture

What the story-telling method is to children, the lecture method is to adults. It permits the presentation of the lesson to a class of unlimited numbers, and permits close adherence to the teacher's preparation. It makes possible an uninterrupted and properly connected discourse leading up to a practical conclusion. Like the story-telling method, it acceptably serves the expository mode of procedure. Both time and effort are saved when the teacher is afforded full opportunity to present his preparation, for there are no minutes wasted getting to the point or in waiting for some slow-responding pupil. Moreover, there is no danger of a carefully prepared lesson getting sidetracked by an unexpected suggestion from some member of the class. The lecture method permits a smooth, easy, direct, and systematic development of the lesson.

But all of the above advantages are lost if the class is not closely following the lecturer and thinking with him. And it is quite possible they will not be. Some members of the class may sit perfectly passive, taking no thought of the lesson during the lecture, and doing nothing about it afterward. Mental and spiritual as well as physical growth come through activity. And this activity can be insured only when the pupil is expected to take part in or contribute to the development of the lesson.

So serious are the limitations of the lecture method that it must be put down as the least to be preferred, and should be used only when the brevity of time and the large number to be reached demand a direct discourse. Only teachers who possess strong personalities and are capable of winning and holding the undivided attention of the class will achieve success with this method.

QUESTIONS

1. What is the expository mode? State its difficulties.
2. Explain the experience mode and its limitations.
3. How may the difficulties of the expository mode be overcome?
4. Name five methods of development.
5. What is the story-telling method, and in what departments can it be used most effectively?
6. What are the four elements of a good story?
7. What is the recitation method and where should it be largely used?
8. Point out four advantages of the recitation method.
9. Distinguish between the recitation and discussion methods.
10. a. Why is the discussion method the most nearly ideal?
    b. Upon what does its success depend?
11. a. What is the research method?
    b. How can it be made effective?
12. What are the advantages and disadvantages of the lecture method?

18

Procedure

WE HAVE observed that the preparation of the lesson involves much more than a study of the Scripture passages that are to be considered the following Sunday. Success in the presentation of the lesson in reality depends upon three steps in preparation.

1. Training of the teacher

In an early chapter stress was laid upon the preparation of the teacher for his task. Even the reception of a certificate or a diploma does not permanently qualify him for his work. The fact is, one cannot be a teacher unless he is a learner. When a teacher ceases to be a learner, he ceases to be a teacher. If he studies he will inspire others to study. Pupils prefer to drink from running brooks and not stagnant pools. It is encumbent upon the teacher constantly to tap new reservoirs of teaching material and teaching methods.

2. Assembling of lesson material

This we know is a perennial task. In his vast field of research, the teacher

> "Finds tongues in trees, books in the running brooks,
> Sermons in stones, and good in everything."

His selections will be guided and governed by the needs of his pupils as they are manifested from week to week in his close intercourse and acquaintance with them.

3. Organizing the lesson material

This we have observed is a specific preparation for a designated lesson, simplified in scope and multiplied in efficiency through relationship to preceding steps. This final stage of preparation, which will be approached with confidence if not with anticipation because of the earlier effort that has been put forth, will likewise determine whether the teaching of the lesson is to be drudgery or joy. For the well-trained and carefully prepared teacher, conducting the lesson is really a simple and satisfactory procedure. Adequate time and thought given to *planning the work,* leaves the teacher to *work the plan.*

The teacher who has put into practice the principles we have been considering will come to realize that the success of their application depends largely on many seemingly insignificant details, which are of great importance.

Before we consider the presentation of the lesson to the class, it would be well to review the seven laws of teaching which were studied. All of these principles, with the possible exception of the first, are applicable to the class period. They will need to be observed if success is to attend our efforts.

The lesson period itself may be considered under four successive steps:

I. APPROACHING THE LESSON

The first few minutes of a battle have decided the issue frequently. Upon the opening of the lesson often hinges success or failure. Upon the spirit and method of the attack rest the results that follow. The most carefully laid plans may avail nothing because of failure in the attack. Before any reference whatever is made to the lesson, it is well to observe that the first concern is the *attitude* and *interest* of the pupils.

1. Welcome pupils

The campaign to win the attention and interest of the pupils begins the moment they reach class. If the teacher is in his place five to ten minutes before the opening of the session, there will be time for a personal greeting as each member of the class arrives. A tardy teacher is at a disadvantage. Aside from the realization that at the very start he is on the defensive, he is not in position to give the individual welcome to each pupil. Furthermore, the pupil's response to his reception is important in that it will be an index to his personal attitude to the lesson period and what the teacher may expect from him in the way of attention.

2. Contact with class

The average boy as he comes to class is not thinking of what will be taught. How then may a right attitude on the part of the pupil be secured? By entering into his interests sufficiently to win his confidence and attention, so that he may be easily led to the lesson plane. If the pupil does not "attend with interest to the lesson to be learned," it is useless to proceed. Arousing real interest is the only successful method of overcoming inattention and preventing disorder.

a. Topic of the day

The teacher may successfully solicit attention by referring to some recent event familiar to most of the class. With older pupils who read the newspapers, there will be a wide field of interest; but with younger children, some happening in their school or play life will probably strike an immediate response. Teachers who make it a point to be closely informed, if not associated with the weekday activities of the pupils, will have no difficulty at this point.

b. Story

With younger pupils a story will frequently serve to arouse and sustain attention, and with little children a picture or an object will gain immediate response through the eye-gate. Dr. McKinney suggests that the lesson period begin with an illustration drawn from the everyday experience of the pupil, "to attract his attention, on the one hand, and to impress the truth which the teacher wishes to leave in his mind, on the other hand." [1]

c. Reports of assignments

Pupils are always interested in their own activities, and unless the home work they have prepared has a definite place in the later development of the lesson, it would be well to start out with a report of their assignments. Unless they are recognized and commended in this work, little can be expected of the pupils outside of class; if the first attention of the class can be directed to it, its significance and importance will be emphasized.

II. OPENING THE LESSON

Having gained the pupils' attention, the next problem is to hold it. First of all, before proceeding with the lesson, let us remember that attention cannot be maintained without interest, and interest is never sustained in a subject which the mind does not grasp. It is essential that we start with familiar ground, remembering the new can be comprehended only in terms of the old.

1. Contact with lesson

Before introducing the lesson of the day, it would be well to:

a. Relate it to previous lessons

The lesson of the day is but a chapter in a complete revelation that God has given, and a close relationship to all pre-

[1] McKinney, *Practical Pedagogy in the Sunday School*, p. 81.

ceding chapters is vital if the interest of the pupil is to be sustained and his understanding furthered. The Bible tells a human story that has a beginning and an ending, and it means much for the pupil to know just what place the lesson has in that story.

b. Relate it to the last lesson

The pupils will probably have a better memory of the last lesson than of previous study, so it can be dwelt upon a little more fully, especially that portion which most vitally associates it with the day's lesson. We never gain time by omitting a review. More real progress can be made in twenty minutes after five minutes has been spent making a point of contact, than in a half hour's effort to comprehend an unconnected lesson.

Perhaps the chief requirement is that the teacher vary the ways in which he conducts a review so as to avoid the listlessness that comes from knowing what to expect.

2. Announce subject

This should not be a formal statement that the topic of the lesson is so and so, which soon becomes monotonous, but rather what interesting information will be disclosed today in the light of what was learned the previous week. Unfortunately, those who prepare our lesson topics do not always take the pupil's interest into consideration, therefore the teacher should make the topic of the lesson attract as much attention as the headlines of a newspaper.

3. Announce object

There is difference of opinion whether it is wise for the teacher to disclose his aim at the beginning. Often an application can be made more effectively if the pupil is not warned in advance. On the other hand, the object of temperance, missionary, or other lessons that have been placed in the curriculum for a specific purpose, can be announced in advance.

4. Announce outline

If the teacher is not likely to follow his outline, it would be a mistake to reveal it, but on the other hand, like the lead in a newspaper item, there is value in presenting a leading thought in an opening paragraph to arouse interest in what is to follow.

III. DEVELOPING THE LESSON

"Well begun is half done." Having completely won the interest and attention of the pupil, and having successfully introduced him to the lesson, the teacher has but to proceed with his preparation. The rule is to *develop the outline of the lesson by methods chosen through examination, illustration, and application of the teaching material.* The actual teaching of the lesson will show far better than any suggestions how far the preparation has been of value, and how far the method is the one best for present use.

Many things must be kept in mind as the teacher proceeds with the lesson, but most of all he must ever remember that "one does not actually teach unless he causes someone to know something which he has not known," and that the real test of a teacher's work is not what he says, but what his pupils remember. Therefore he must constantly

1. Stimulate thought

For this purpose the question will be found to be the most valuable weapon, and the teacher who develops the lesson by a series of thought-provoking inquiries will never fail to accomplish his purpose. Information should not be imparted without asking for it again in some form. Some information, of course, must be given, but good teaching requires that the pupil's mind be constantly tested to see if he is alert and if he has actually profited by what has been told him. It is well to remember that if questions are to be employed effectively and extensively, progress will be slow, and the same amount of ground cannot be covered as if the story-telling or lecture method were used to present the material. Time is required to give pupils an opportunity to think, but until they think, all the instruction imparted has little value.

If one teaches entirely through the use of questions, it is essential that his outline be kept well in mind. The pupils should recognize the pathway of thought as the lesson is developed, and should realize that they are making definite progress despite the questioning process. It is a good plan after the first fact of the outline has been developed through questions, to briefly sum up the results of the class work in positive form, and then proceed to the next, and so on to the end. Most illustrations, unless familiar, will have to be introduced by direct statement, but the teacher can always ask the class to suggest some application of the lesson truth before offering his own.

2. Reproduce thought

Since what the pupil expresses is most likely to be remembered, it is fully as important that he be encouraged to reproduce his thoughts as that he be stimulated to think. As Miss Plummer notes:

"In all teaching it is well to use regularly the 'telling back' plan. Adults greatly profit by this method; with children it is essential. Never tell your class what you can induce them to tell you. Here is a common mistake. The teacher should use all his powers of diplomacy in getting a pupil to put into words that which his mind grasps. It is worth infinitely more to a pupil to tell some truth, even in a broken, bungling way, than to have you tell it beautifully and eloquently. When he can tell it, he knows it. He may hear you tell it many times without knowing it. Trying to tell it helps him to know it." [2]

[2] Plummer, *The Soul-Winning Teacher,* p. 77.

But beyond the reproduction of the facts of the lesson—and this is the starting point—the teacher should strive to have the pupil express *himself*—give *his* interpretation and *his* application of the lesson. It is this great failure of the teaching ministry that has led modern educators to promote experience-centered lessons. However, it should not be necessary for any one to abandon truth and cease to make it central in instruction in order that pupils may do their own thinking. Pupils can be trained to base their experience on biblical truth. Expressional activities should be introduced in the Beginners department and continued thereafter during the years the child is in Sunday school. Only lessons that contain expressional activities should be admitted in the curriculum. With this constant emphasis on the application, as well as the acquisition, of knowledge, especially in the early years, pupils will come actually to expect the teacher to stand aside so that they can participate in the lesson.

IV. CLOSING THE LESSON

The lesson should not be ended abruptly or without a fitting conclusion. As careful consideration needs to be given to the finish as to the start. From three to five minutes need to be reserved for this purpose.

1. Recapitulation

Perhaps the outline, if fully followed, will suggest the best summary of the lesson. If the questions of the pupils or the trend of class discussion have not made it possible to adhere closely to the outline, the teacher in any event, should sum up the net results of the class period. What are the fundamental facts brought out in the discussion of which the pupils should be reminded?

And with the recapitulation of the lesson facts will be associated the important truths that have been introduced. What important lesson will the pupil carry with him? What final application should be made? The lesson has been taught; has Christ been revealed as the Saviour of sinners? If not, could a more practical application be made in conclusion?

2. The next lesson

Before the class is dismissed, the teacher will want to give some thought to the next lesson.

a. Arouse interest

The teacher not only desires the class to return the following Sunday, but to come back with expectation. By some startling statement or striking question, curiosity and interest can be aroused in what will be taken up the next week. As a writer by a fascinating conclusion leads his readers to look forward to the next chapter of a serial story, so a teacher should strive to finish the day's portion of "the most interesting story in the world" with such a climactic ending that the entire class will look forward to the next Sunday's installment.

b. Make assignments

These should already have been selected during the preparation of the lesson, but the animated way in which the part is assigned to the individual pupil will determine the interest and enthusiasm with which he will enter upon his task.

QUESTIONS

1. Upon what three steps in preparation does the success of the lesson depend?
2. What are the four successive steps to be followed in the presentation of the lesson?
3. Suggest three ways in which the teacher may make a point of contact with the class.
4. What four steps are to be taken in opening the lesson?
5. Why is it necessary to relate the lesson to previous lessons as well as to the last lesson?

6. Discuss the wisdom of announcing the object of the lesson.
7. State the rule for the development of the lesson.
8. What allowance must be made if questions are used to stimulate thought?
9. How may questions be used to stimulate thought without departing from the outline?
10. What attention should be given to the reproduction of thought?
11. Make some suggestions for the recapitulation of the lesson.
12. What two considerations should be given to the next lesson?

19

Observation and Practice Teaching

WHILE there is much that can be learned from textbooks on pedagogy, its principles can be made permanent by observation and practice teaching.

I. OBSERVATION

Visit some class where there is good teaching, and carefully study what goes on. Observe what the teacher does, how he does it, what the pupils do. Note the place, equipment, arrangement, materials. Watch the teacher's attitudes. By observing others, you may receive more vital instruction than from a textbook.

The great difficulty will be to find teachers who are sufficiently well-trained as to afford a good example. It will be of no help to copy mistakes. For this reason, a student who is sent out to observe another teacher at work should be prepared to be a critic. He should have a definite schedule which he can follow. That you may understand the nature of this schedule and how it was used by one of my students in the Christian Education Course, the written report made will be inserted at this point. The assignment was to the Intermediate department of the Sunday school in one of the city churches, and the criticism concerns the platform exercises of the *departmental* session, as well as the class period.

1. Physical conditions

   a. Ventilation

The facilities for proper ventilation were splendid—two large French windows on the east side. The room was airy, sunny, and very pleasant.

   b. Temperature

Normal—68°

   c. Seating arrangement

This conformed to a certain adopted principle—boys on one side and girls on the other. The diagram on an adjoining page will show how well the room was arranged, and how it was so satisfactory for the worship period.

   d. Handicaps

In a way the room was all that could be desired. It was pleasant, inviting, and conducive to worship. The large vase of colorful flowers on the piano, the floor lamp, flowered drapes and two beautiful pictures (Christ in the Temple and The Good Shepherd) hanging on the wall, gave the room a homelike atmosphere.

The room was unsatisfactory for the lesson period however. The department consisted of two classes of boys and three classes of girls. For the lesson period, the two boys' classes adjourned to the rooms adjoining the Department. The girls' classes remained in the larger room; curtains were drawn to separate the three groups while in class session. The hum of voices was audible throughout the lesson teaching.

I sat with the class at the rear of the room. I saw the various intrusions, the elements that disturbed the progress of the lesson. Two secretaries worked at a desk nearby. Their conversation, the jingling of coins, the walking to and fro from

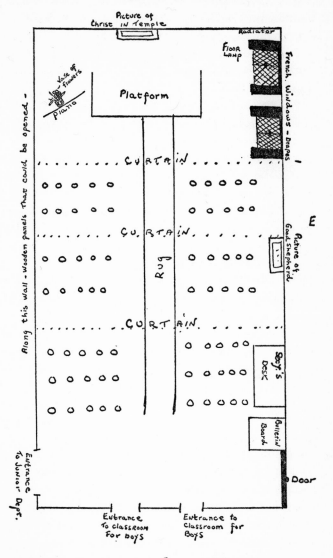

the classrooms, certainly did not help the situation. All in all, it was a difficult atmosphere in which to teach.

Furthermore, the comparatively small space did not permit blackboard work or any type of handwork that required a board.

2. Worship program

The service started promptly at the appointed hour. A man from another department led the singing, and a young woman played the piano. The song leader announced the opening hymn, "Jesus Is All the World to Me," which was followed by the raising of hands asking for certain favorites. One of the boys requested "We've a Story to Tell to the Nations," and another boy asked for "Holy, Holy, Holy." The final hymn was chosen by a girl,—"All the Way My Saviour Leads Me."

At the close of the song service, the leader left and a young woman took charge. She announced the Scripture portion, which was read by one of the girls. I was a little disturbed to notice a boy taking the register for his class to the secretary's desk during the reading of the Word of God.

Following the Scripture reading, a special musical number was announced. A young man from another department sang, "Morning," by Oley Speaks. This was beautifully done, but it seemed to me inappropriate in a worship service. It did not correlate with the theme of the lesson. The offering was taken after the solo.

The most uplifting moment of the service came when the woman in charge called on one of the boys (about eleven years of age) to lead in prayer. This was most impressive. He prayed for the members of the church, those outside the church, the missionaries, and finally for the nation and those in authority.

The worship service was nicely arranged, but I could not

help questioning whether or not the pupils had grasped the full significance of worship and reverence. Seated in the rear of the room, I could see that several children were talking during the program.

After the lesson period, the classes again assembled in the Department room. The acting superintendent called on a ten-year-old boy to announce a meeting of a certain boys' organization in the church. This was well done, and the boy gave promise of ability as a leader. Then the group was dismissed with prayer.

3. Routine

a. Record making

The registers were marked during the worship period. In two of the classes, a pupil did the marking. Some registers were picked up by one of the secretaries immediately after the classes adjourned for the lesson period.

b. Distribution of materials

Registers were distributed during the song service. Sunday school papers were given out at the close of the session, as the pupils filed past the secretaries' desk.

c. Entrance and exit of pupils

There was no difficulty in this regard, for the entrance was at the rear of the room and tardy children could slip in quietly. The boys, since they did not remain in the room for the lesson period, sat near the front; but the girls sat in their respective classes, and it was impossible for the girls who were late to slip in without being observed and disturbing others in case of no vacant seats.

4. Personal factors in teaching

a. Appearance

I trust I am being fair in judgment when I say that this teacher did not measure up to the standards for her position.

Both dress and extremely unnatural coloring attracted undue attention to herself.

b. Voice

This teacher had a rather pleasant voice, but it was much too weak. Since I was sitting near her, I could hear, but the noise from the lesson taught in the other classes was distracting. Her tempo was good, and the pitch with intermingled inflections pleasing.

c. Mannerisms

Since the teacher sat in the circle with her class, it was difficult to note mannerisms. She kept the same pose throughout the lesson—sitting with legs crossed, book in hand.

d. Personality

She had a pleasing personality, and at times showed real animation in her teaching. Her lack of confidence was in evidence, doubtless attributable to my presence. With lack of ease she could not give herself wholly to the lesson. I admired her tact and patience with the pupils when they could not answer her questions. She did not allow the noise from the other classes to distract her. Although her lack of knowledge in spiritual matters was evident, she showed promise as a teacher.

e. Attitude

There was real effort to reach the pupils, but they did not respond very well. Had this teacher had more of a Bible background, she could have shown more enthusiasm for the lesson. I am sure that she would be most willing to be taught in the Scriptures and in methods of teaching.

5. **Pupils' behavior**

a. Attention

The girls were courteous, but the least sound diverted their attention. While they sat passively, they gained little from the lesson, as the questionnaire at the close revealed.

b. Interest

Since the pupils did not participate in the lesson, they were not vitally interested. They did not give the teacher their undivided attention, and the lesson did not seem to have anything for them personally.

c. Manners

This group was well-mannered; judging from their dress and behavior in the class, they had come from good homes. They did not talk during the lesson; they were intelligent enough, but the teacher just did not win their interest.

d. Regularity

The Department had a total membership of 56. On the day of my visit, there were 36 members and 7 visitors present.

e. Punctuality

For the most part, this was not a problem in the Department. The majority came on time; two boys were a few minutes late.

f. Initiative

Only two girls, out of the class of ten, showed initiative or made any attempt to answer a few of the questions. On one occasion, one of the girls endeavored to give an opinion. She was the only one who did so; the others remained silent and content to let the teacher do the talking.

g. Co-operation

There was apparent lack of real co-operation between teacher and pupil. I am inclined to believe that it was because the teacher failed to interest the girls in the lesson.

6. **The teacher**

a. Preparation

Lack of preparation was evident and this lack was admitted by the teacher. When I was introduced to her, she said in the presence of the pupils, "I felt rather badly about your being present this morning, for I have not prepared the lesson."

b. Plan

The teacher had neither outline nor aim. I believe that reading the lesson once or twice constituted the preparation. There was no opening prayer. The approach was made by asking the girls to read the lesson through—each one reading a verse.

c. Application

No application was made to include experiences or problems with which the girls would have been familiar. The application which was made was not suitable; it could have been given to juniors or adults with the same results. Without an aim or a plan one can understand the inability to make a worthwhile application.

d. Method

The lack of interest and co-operation on the part of the pupils forced the teacher to do practically all of the talking. She did not make use of stories, similes, or practical applications, but gave an exposition of the Scripture verse by verse.

e. Class participation

Judging from the inability of the pupils to answer questions it seemed certain they had not studied the lesson. One girl answered two questions and volunteered an opinion on a third; another girl answered one question, but that was the extent of the pupil activity during the lesson. The questions were directed to the group instead of being directed to individuals.

Toward the close of the class session the attention of the girls was directed to the questionnaire at the bottom of the page of the lesson sheet in the manual. Mentioning those questions was the only recitation for that class period, with only a few participating.

7. Sundry remarks

This experience was not only interesting, it was intensely helpful. It did much to impress me with the soundness of my own classroom training and work along these lines.

An explanation needs to be added lest the report given appear too critical. At the close of the class period, we were introduced to the regular superintendent of the department, and she explained that the teacher in whose class we have been seated had accepted the class for that particular Sunday only. What a need for teacher-training was shown to me that day! The young lady asked to teach had accepted with the admission to me that she had not prepared for the lesson. Another thing which this young woman told me was, "I can't find words to express myself." Some expressions she used seemed to be far removed from the requirement of the sacred Scriptures. The foundation upon which she built the lesson was weakened greatly by a lack of positiveness which could have been given in Scripture itself. There was a *hope* expressed of reaching heaven in this way: "Heaven is prepared for people who believe Christ, I *hope* to go there some day." With regard to prayer there was this statement: "When we are in trouble we get down on our knees and pray, *hoping* that God will answer our prayer." Proper Christian training would change a teacher like that to one able to point the way to Christ, heaven, and answers to prayers, all to the eternal blessing of the pupils entrusted to her care.

II. PRACTICE TEACHING

All students who attend normal schools are accustomed to practice teaching. It is recognized as one of the most practical ways in which one can learn how to teach. Probably there is no subject in which the pupil is more influenced by the teacher than pedagogy. Attention has already been called to the importance of the teacher's personality—that he himself is the greatest visual aid that can ever be presented to a class.

No one can develop skill in teaching without practice. One can learn to do well only by doing. Mere practice, however, never makes perfect. Unless it is practice of the right procedure it will be clumsy, wasteful, and imperfect. One must practice on the basis of accurate knowledge, with adequate provision for constant correction and improvement. Constructive criticism by another, especially if he be experienced in teaching, will be of great value in connection with practice. Both the teacher and his critic must conform to well-recognized principles. This removes any possibility of personal prejudice, or an individualistic viewpoint. The individual who practices should have the information and know the standards needed for criticism. In the last analysis, all criticism must become self-criticism. For only as one accepts the criticism graciously and heeds its suggestions will it be of any value.

1. Teaching

Where I taught for years, one of the most popular and practical classes in the Christian Education Course was Practice Teaching. Everyone in the class was expected to teach twice, so that there would be good opportunity to observe improvement. The teaching material was the Bible Units of the Preliminary Course of the Evangelical Teacher Training Association in use for three reasons:

a. The class was composed of young people of the age for which the manuals had been written.

b. The contents of the course served as a survey and review of the Bible knowledge the student had acquired.

c. The manuals constituted the teaching material that these students would use in training classes.

The student was given one-half hour in which to present his lesson. Not only was he required to begin promptly, but also to find good terminals for completing his presentation. In his preparation he would provide contacts with the pupil and with previous lessons. He would prepare a list of questions in order that his ability to awaken and direct thought might be tested. He would also secure some good illustrations, and especially for this age, historical, geographical, and literary illustrations. He was also expected to reserve sufficient time for a recapitulation and arousing interest in and making assignments for the next lesson.

Toward the end of the term, it was customary to have at least one composite lesson. All of the students were required to prepare for this occasion, though none of them knew who was going to teach, or at what time during the lesson he would make his contribution. The presentation was largely to test the student's ability to fit his instruction in with the teaching of those who had preceded, and of those who would follow him. He had to keep in mind not only the point to which the lesson should have progressed at the time he was called upon, but also that his contribution should not introduce so many details as to make it difficult for subsequent teachers to complete the lesson in the time remaining.

2. Criticism

In one sense, all of the class were critics, as they would have to divide their attention between the presentation of the lesson and criticizing the observance of one of the laws of teaching. In addition, if the class were sufficiently large, eight of the number served as judges. Each was a critic who gave his entire time to criticizing the observance of one of the eight laws. They were not called upon to recite, so they could give their undivided attention to criticism. The seven laws of Gregory were the standard by which criticisms were made, and there was added what was called the law of personality, in which the appearance, voice, gestures, and animation of the teacher were criticized.

As soon as a student had completed his assignment in teaching, he was responsible for the law of the personality. At the next session, he began to judge the instructor by the law of the teacher. And then, on successive days, his assignment was the law of the pupil, the language, the lesson, the question, the response, and the recapitulation.

At the conclusion of the teaching, we listened to the reports of the eight judges. In addition to the verbal presentation in class, the students were required to write their criticisms later and hand them in. The verbal report occupied fifteen minutes. This allowed me ten minutes to pass on the merits of the teaching, and especially to criticize the reports of the judges.

3. Examination

How could a class like this, that is being constantly tested, have a final examination? This was not difficult to arrange. As the classes generally were so large that it was impossible to have all of the students teach twice in one term, the new students were not required to teach the first term. As members of the class, they were merely observers. However, they constituted excellent material with which to conduct a final examination. At the last session, these new students were given their first opportunity to teach. No one knew who would be called on, or just when. Moreover, to give as large a number as possible an opportunity to appear before the class, no one would teach more than three or four minutes. Meanwhile, the others were carefully noting the strong and weak points of each teacher, so they could later go to their rooms and prepare their appraisement of the teaching ability of each one who had participated. Thus far, the class had concentrated its criticism upon one person and then observance of only one law. In this final test, they were required to observe a group of teachers and all of the laws of teaching.

QUESTIONS

1. Why should observation and practice teaching be essential in a course of pedagogy?
2. What are some of the difficulties in observation?

3. Prepare a diagram of the department, noting windows, piano, platform, exits, and arrangement of classes.
4. What points should the observer note about the physical conditions?
5. What three things should be noted in the routine?
6. Name five personal factors to be observed in teaching.
7. In what seven respects is the pupils' behavior to be criticized?
8. Name five points for judging the teacher.
9. What is the value of practice teaching?
10. Explain the plan followed in my Christian Education Course classes.
11. What arrangements were made for criticisms?
12. How was the final examination conducted?

Part VI: *The Model Teacher*

20

The Master Teacher

NO ONE can make a careful study of the Gospels without coming to the realization that our Lord Jesus Christ was the master teacher, and was not only the master teacher, but the master of all teaching. He did not establish a system of teaching. Nevertheless, it is well to note to what extent He appears to have observed modern laws of pedagogy.

I. THE TEACHER

We who believe the truths of Scripture, of course realize that Jesus cannot be regarded as an ordinary person. He was, as Peter confessed, truly the Son of God. As such He must be conceded supernatural knowledge and power. However, in considering His life as a teacher we must not overlook His humanity. Though He was equal with God, He chose to make Himself "of no reputation, and took upon him the form of a servant, and was made in the likeness of men" (Phil. 2:6, 7). Therefore, it is only from a consideration of His life from the human side that it would be possible in any way to evaluate His teaching methods.

1. His preparation

In no other country has the art of teaching been so magnified as in Palestine. In no other country has a teacher ever attained to such an exalted position. Jesus was born at a time and in a place where the honor due to a teacher bordered on reverence. While we are not told that He went to school, it cannot be doubted that He did go. His parents' knowledge of the all-important place He was to take in life makes it reasonable to believe that they gave Him every opportunity their limited means would permit, to fit Him for His ministry. Moreover, the fact that He did not enter into His life work until He was thirty would indicate that ample time was provided. However, He was not, like Paul, a student of one of the great teachers of the day (Acts 22:3); nor did He receive recognition as having completed a prescribed course, as John 7:15 suggests. When the Jews marveled at His teaching ability, and exclaimed, "How knoweth this man letters, having never learned?" they voiced their astonishment that He should demonstrate such exceptional ability without having completed the preparatory course they deemed essential. His education, from the human standpoint, may be summed up as follows:

a. He was a master of the art of reading

This was demonstrated when He went into the synagogue at Nazareth and was given the Book of Isaiah from which to read the lesson of the day.

b. He was familiar with the less common art of writing

His allusions to the forms of the Hebrew letters (Matt. 5:18), and His writing with His finger on the ground (John 8:6), are conclusive evidence on that point.

c. He knew Hebrew as well as the Aramaic dialect

Long before this, the Hebrew language had become a dead letter. The common people spoke the Aramaic dialect, but the Old Testament was written in Hebrew, and in Greek (Septuagint).

d. He was profoundly versed in the Scripture

Again and again in His controversies with the rabbis, He would throw out a challenge to their scholarship—"Have ye not read?" This thorough knowledge of the Scripture was the content of the instruction in the Jewish school, and it is evident that as a boy our Lord was not only a faithful attendant, but a zealous student of the law, and like His associates committed vast portions of it to memory.

e. He was familiar with the traditions

This is evident from what we read of His controversies with the Jews (Matt. 15:1–20).[1]

2. His convictions

He was not primarily an orator, reformer, or ruler, but rather a teacher. Evidence could be multiplied that Jesus regarded Himself as a teacher.[2] We have the direct statement that He made to His disciples: "Ye call me Master [Teacher] and Lord: and ye say well; for so I am" (John 13:13). The entire Gospel record assumes that Jesus regarded Himself as a teacher. He went frequently into synagogues and temple for the evident purpose of teaching. Teaching was His chief business. Jesus thoroughly believed in teaching—an indispensable prerequisite for any teacher. He gave Himself to it, and forever dignified the calling. The supreme glory of the teaching profession consists in the fact that when our Lord faced His life work He chose to be a teacher. He was the embodiment of His profession. He assumed a pedagogic authority different from that of the scribes and rabbis, the official teachers of the times. Their authority was based upon knowledge largely from without—what they had been taught. His was from within, and needed not the support of the authorities. He quoted nobody. His own word was offered as sufficient. Therefore, the people were astonished at His teaching. Never before had they listened to messages given with such assurance. Instead of asking support for His position by an

---

[1] B. A. Hinsdale, *Jesus As a Teacher*, p. 37.
[2] C. F. McKoy, *The Art of Jesus As a Teacher*, p. 24.

appeal to the tradition of the elders, He shows their inconsistencies and shortcomings.

Living what He taught inspired confidence in His statements. People saw embodied in His teachings what He sought to have them to do. They observed how He experienced sorrow, criticism, disappointment, persecution. His living re-enforced and gave weight to what He said. No other teacher ever exhibited such poise in any classroom. He never appeared at a disadvantage. He was never taken unawares. Although beset by the scribes, Pharisees and Sadducees, He maintained the equilibrium of His disposition. He never lost control of any situation. In every instance He remained master of the field.

3. His recognition

When our Lord entered upon His public ministry, He is spoken of again and again as *teaching* in the synagogues, as distinct from *preaching* in them. While John the Baptist is represented only as a preacher, Christ is repeatedly spoken of as teacher (Matt. 4:23; 9:35; 11:1; Mark 1:21, 22; Luke 20:1). The question, "How knoweth this man letters, having never learned?" (John 7:15), was not asked concerning John the Baptist, but concerning Jesus, because He occupied the more important place of teacher—questioning His pupils and answering their inquiries. The proof that our Lord was recognized as a teacher may be set forth under five heads:

a. The name by which He was addressed

Out of ninety times, in sixty He was given the title, "Teacher." Even in the thirty other titles He was given, it is evident that most of them indicate a teaching rather than a preaching ministry.

b. The name by which His followers were known

They were called disciples or learners, and their entire attitude was that of pupils.

c. The comparatively large amount of time He spent in instructing His disciples.

From the time He introduced the parables, He gave almost exclusive attention to the training of His disciples. His contacts with the multitude, His public miracles and parables, were used as a means for illustrating and illuminating His instruction for His disciples.

d. The method He employed in dealing with large groups

In His controversies with the Herodians, Sadducees, and Pharisees, His frequent use of the question is evidence that He was a teacher.

e. The employment of the word teach *in the Great Commission*

Not only did Jesus regard teaching as one of the principal factors of His ministry, but He commissioned His disciples to go forth and teach also. They were to contact all nations, teaching them to observe all things whatsoever He had commanded them (Matt. 28:19). It may well be asked, in this connection, if the Christian church has sufficiently emphasized the teaching ministry of our Lord.

He was recognized as a teacher, despite the fact that He departed from the customary place as well as methods in teaching. The rabbis restricted their instruction to the school and the synagogue. Our Lord taught in the temple, and on the mountain, by the seaside, by the road, by the well, in the home.[3] The Gospel writer says He went all over Galilee, teaching in their synagogues and curing any disease or sickness among the people (Matt. 4:23). The atmosphere of a school predominated, for the people felt free to ask Him questions, and He in turn asked them questions.

[3] J. M. Price, *Jesus the Teacher*, p. 7.

II. THE CHARACTER OF HIS TEACHING

So much attention has been given to what our Lord taught that the manner in which He presented His instruction has been largely overlooked. Even from the limited material given us in the Gospels, it is not difficult to recognize in our Lord a master teacher. He knew His subjects. The most prolific cause of failure among teachers, next to the inability to discipline, is the lack of thorough knowledge of the subject taught. Christ knew His teaching material perfectly. Moreover, His teaching was not a pouring in, but rather a pumping out, process. He did not do ninety-nine per cent of the talking Himself. Instead, He invited discussion and gave the class an opportunity to contribute and participate. He organized His material psychologically rather than logically. The needs of the pupils were put above the demands of the subject matter, and He adapted His teaching of the truth to the action or the question of the moment. He saw to it that His pupils mastered their subject. He taught them a few things at a time, and He repeated His instruction until He was assured that it had been not only acquired but assimilated. He taught leisurely. He never was in a hurry. He selected the most important principles and emphasized them. Three observations should be made of His teaching:

1. His mastery of Scripture

In the Gospels, which record only a brief portion of our Lord's ministry, it is significant that He quoted from at least sixteen books of the Old Testament. He not only knew the Scriptures, but had assimilated them to such an extent that He could apply them to any situation which might arise. He was not only able to hold His own with the doctors in the temple, at the age of twelve, but with the most severe critics at all times. His mastery of Scripture was demonstrated on the following occasions:

a. The temptation in the wilderness

Our Lord met each of the three temptations to which He was subjected with an appropriate answer from the Book of Deuteronomy. When Satan attempted to quote Scripture for his purpose, our Lord proved His superior knowledge and resourcefulness with an effective counter quotation, and the enemy of God and the adversary of man was obliged to abandon the field.

b. The sermon in Nazareth

At the very beginning of His ministry, Jesus paid a visit to His home town, Nazareth, "and, as his custom was, he went into the synagogue on the sabbath day, and stood up for to read" (Luke 4:16). The visiting Preacher was given the scroll containing the prophecy of Isaiah. He quickly found the place (Isa. 61:1) where centuries before the prophet had predicted His ministry. Without comment of any kind, our Lord announced, after He had concluded the striking prophecy concerning Himself, "This day is this scripture fulfilled in your ears" (Luke 4:21).

Instead of feeling honored, the people of His village were angered at this declaration, and it was necessary for our Lord to quote further Scripture to prove that God's sovereign grace is for those whom He chooses. He reminded His hearers of the widow of Sarepta, to whom alone Elijah was sent in the time of famine. Then He spake of Naaman the Syrian, who alone of all the lepers of his time was cleansed through the ministry of Elijah. His complete knowledge of Scripture enabled Him not only to recall the passages that were appropriate for meeting the situation, but also to wield the Word of God as a mighty sword, to strike the truth home to the hearts of His hearers.

264 *The Christian Teacher*

c. The Sabbath controversy

The Pharisees, who were very punctilious for the observance of the letter of law, criticized the disciples for plucking the ears of corn on the Sabbath day. Jesus answered His critics from the very law that they claimed His disciples had broken. He reminded them of what David did when he and his followers were hungry on the Sabbath day. He also referred to the custom of the priests in the temple, "who profane the sabbath and are blameless." As a culmination to these Scripture illustrations, which showed the Pharisees their ignorance of the real spirit of the law, the Master Teacher proclaimed Himself as "Lord even of the sabbath day" (Matt. 12:1–8). Not only was the law made for the benefit of man, and not man for the law, but Christ Himself was the Author of the law, and could make what alterations He chose.

d. The post-resurrection instruction

Probably at no time did our Lord so exhibit His mastery of Scripture as in those days He spent with His disciples after His resurrection. To Cleopas and his companion who were journeying to Emmaus on the afternoon of the resurrection day, a Stranger appeared and entered into their discussion concerning the mystery of a crucified and risen Messiah. It was only when the Stranger opened up the Scriptures and expounded to them the many prophecies concerning Himself, that the mystery was explained (Luke 24:13–27).

Later in the evening of the same day, He appeared to the disciples in an upper room, and quieted their fears not only by showing them the wounds in His hands and His feet, but by rehearsing in their ears the things "written in the law of Moses, and in the prophets, and in the psalms" concerning Himself (Luke 24:33–45). He had told them much about Himself, and after the Old Testament passages were rehearsed in their ears, we read, "Then opened he their understanding, that they might understand the scriptures."

2. His knowledge of human nature

Our Lord's understanding of human nature was an important factor in His successful use of the Scriptures. He not only understood the Jewish mind in general, as to factions and sects, but He also was a master in penetrating the heart and understanding the inner workings of the individual mind.[4] While our recognition of our Lord's deity would require that we admit His omniscience, nevertheless we can observe even from the human standpoint that He was a master of psychology. From the outset, He loved all His pupils, not merely the lovable or the bright ones, but even the unlovable. He never held a grudge against a pupil for some past conduct. It was the disciple who denied Him thrice that He particularly sought out after His resurrection and commanded to feed His lambs. He was more swift to commend than to condemn. He commended Peter particularly when he made his great confession of faith, and refrained from criticizing his blunders (Matt. 16:17; John 18:10, 11).

a. He knew the minds of His disciples

On one occasion, when the disciples complained at His saying that they must eat of His flesh and drink of His blood, in order to have life, Jesus knowing in Himself that His disciples murmured at Him, said to them, "Doth this offend you? What and if ye shall see the Son of man ascend up where he was before? . . . But there are some of you that believe not. For Jesus knew from the beginning who they were that believed not, and who should betray him" (John 6:60–64).

Shortly after our Lord had come down from the mount of transfiguration, there arose a reasoning among the disciples,

[4] Price, *op. cit.,* p. 10.

which of them should be greatest. It was then that our Lord "perceiving the thought of their heart, took a child, and set him by him. And said unto them, Whosoever shall receive this child in my name receiveth me: and whosoever shall receive me receiveth him that sent me: for he that is least among you all, the same shall be great" (Luke 9:47, 48).

b. Jesus knew the minds of His enemies

When the man sick of the palsy was lowered from the roof of the house into the room where our Lord was ministering, he was greeted with this statement, "Son, be of good cheer; thy sins be forgiven thee." This utterance led certain of the scribes to say within themselves, "This man blasphemeth." But Jesus, knowing their thoughts said, "Wherefore think ye evil in your hearts? For whether is easier, to say, Thy sins be forgiven thee; or to say, Arise, and walk? But that ye may know that the Son of man hath power on earth to forgive sins (then saith he to the sick of the palsy), Arise, take up thy bed, and go unto thine house. And he arose, and departed to his house" (Matt. 9:2–7).

On another occasion, when the scribes and Pharisees were carefully watching our Lord to see whether or not He would heal on the Sabbath day, that they might find an accusation against Him, we read that "He knew their thoughts, and said to the man which had the withered hand, Rise up, and stand forth in the midst. And he arose and stood forth" (Luke 6:6–8).

In the last days of His ministry, when every effort was being made to entangle Him in His talk, the Herodians propounded what they regarded as an unanswerable question, "What thinkest thou? Is it lawful to give tribute unto Caesar, or not? But Jesus perceived their wickedness, and said, Why tempt ye me, ye hypocrites? Show me the tribute money.

And they brought unto him a penny. And he saith unto them, Whose is this image and superscription? They say unto him, Caesar's. Then saith he unto them, Render therefore unto Caesar the things which are Caesar's and unto God the things that are God's" (Matt. 22:16-21).

c. He knew the minds of honest inquirers

Early in His ministry, when He was choosing His disciples, Nathanael accompanied Philip that he might investigate the Man whom the latter claimed was the Messiah. When Jesus saw him coming, He remarked, "Behold an Israelite indeed, in whom is no guile." It was only natural then that Nathanael should inquire, "Whence knowest thou me?" Jesus replied that even before Philip had spoken to him, when he was under the fig tree, He had seen him. Nathanael was evidently surprised to hear this information concerning himself, and the foreknowledge that our Lord exhibited called forth his remarkable confession, "Rabbi, thou art the Son of God; thou art the King of Israel" (John 1:45-49).

In His interview with the Samaritan woman who came to Jacob's well for water, our Lord asked her to call her husband, and when she replied that she had none, He startled her by saying, "Thou hast well said, I have no husband: for thou hast had five husbands; and he whom thou now hast is not thy husband: in that saidst thou truly" (John 4:16-18). No wonder this surprised woman admitted that He was a prophet and later told her friends and neighbors, "Come, see a man, which told me all things that ever I did: is not this the Christ?" (John 4:29). The insight that He portrayed into this woman's character not only convinced her that He was the Messiah, but made her a missionary to the Samaritans of that city, who "believed on him for the saying of the woman, which testified, He told me all that ever I did" (v. 39).

3. His diversified methods

Our Lord was not only unique in His teaching methods, but He was supreme. He employed various forms of teaching as they suited the various relationships in which He stood to His pupils. In general, the stage of enlightenment that His hearers had reached, and their disposition toward Him, determined the method of teaching. He invented nothing new in methods, but used old methods with perfect freedom and efficiency. His originality appears in His mastery of these old methods, in the spirit in which He used them, and in His subject matter.[5]

His instruction looked to a practical end. He expected progress. To this end, He always appealed to the will of His pupils. While the Greek teacher appealed to the reason, and the Roman teacher to the emotional life, Jesus centered His appeal upon the will. There is a fine illustration of this in the closing part of the Sermon on the Mount. Those who hear His Word and do it are wise. Those who hear His Word and do it not are foolish. The whole emphasis rests upon the conduct of the hearer. He was not content to reach the intellect only, but pressed beyond to contact the personality.

Faith must manifest itself in works. This important truth that He taught was fully illustrated in His life. When John the Baptist in his lowly prison, awaiting execution, had begun to question whether after all Jesus was the Messiah, he sent two disciples to interview Him personally. Pushing their way through the crowd that so frequently surrounded our Lord, they asked, "Art thou he that should come, or do we look for another?" The ordinary teacher might have said, "Go back and tell John that everything is all right. He need not worry. I am the Christ." But our Lord understood that this was the time and the opportunity to impress a great truth.

[5] Hinsdale, *op. cit.*, p. 137.

He sent back no word to the melancholy prisoner, but said, "Go and show John again those things which ye do hear and see: the blind receive their sight, and the lame walk, the lepers are cleansed, and the deaf hear, the dead are raised up, and the poor have the gospel preached to them" (Matt. 11:2–5). How forcible this instruction! "Just tell John what you see Me do. Let him judge Me, not by what I say, but by what I do. Let My conduct be My answer."

Jesus had no fixed method in teaching. He was not bound by any routine, or devoted to any system. Rather He was the master of all methods, and varied His process according to the situation He faced and the objective He had in mind. That He was a master of the teaching art is shown by the fact that He used from time to time practically every method that the teaching profession uses today. There were questions, lectures, stories, conversations, discussions, objects, projects, and demonstrations. There were four methods which He seemed to use most:

a. The discourse

This would appear to be a preaching method, and was commonly used in the early part of His ministry, when He was not only making public proclamation of His message, but was preparing His chosen disciples for the more intensive instruction they would receive later. Sometimes it was given to large crowds, and sometimes to small ones. Sometimes all the disciples were present, and at other times a mixed group of friends and enemies. As Dr. David James Burrell says, "His pulpit was often a hillside, or a boat moored by the margin of a lake, His auditorium the blue canopy of the skies, His audience the multitude gathered about Him with faces upturned in eager attention." [6] They called Him, "a teacher come from God."

Three of these discourses occupy more than one chapter

[6] D. J. Burrell, *The Wonderful Teacher,* p. 13.

and are probably the most outstanding. One is on the last judgment, comprising two chapters (Matt. 24 and 25); the longest, the farewell address, filling four chapters in John's Gospel (14–17); the best known, the teaching on the mount, which occupies three chapters (Matt. 5–7).

The Sermon on the Mount, as it is generally erroneously called, was in reality the *teaching* on the mount, because even with this uninterrupted discourse there were the outstanding marks of the teaching profession. In the first place, when the multitudes followed Him up into the mountain, He observed the custom of the rabbis and sat down before He began to teach. Then we are told, "He opened his mouth, and taught them" (Matt. 5:2). Again and again in the discourse, He used the rhetorical question: "Is not the life more than meat, and the body than raiment?" "Which of you by taking thought can add one cubit unto his stature?" "Why beholdest thou the mote that is in thy brother's eye, but considerest not the beam that is in thine own eye?" "Do men gather grapes of thorns, or figs of thistles?" Then at the conclusion of the discourse, we are told that "The people were astonished at his doctrine (teaching): for he taught them as one having authority, and not as the scribes" (Matt. 7:28, 29).

b. The dialogue

In this method, there are two or more speakers. Difficulties are propounded, and efforts made to remove them, all of which gives to the teaching greater variety and animation.[7] The interviews with Nicodemus (John 3), with the woman of Samaria (John 4), and with Simon (Luke 7), are all illustrations of the dialogue. This method also was used when Jesus was teaching His disciples. It served both to instruct the mind and move the heart. In the dialogue there was ample opportunity given for the disciples to ask questions and to

[7] Hinsdale, *op. cit.*, p. 138.

answer the inquiries of the Master. Not only did such questions afford the Saviour an opportunity of imparting more thorough instruction, but those who felt they were well enough acquainted to unburden their hearts to Him were thereby drawn into closer fellowship with Him.

Perhaps one of the best illustrations of the dialogue was the conversation our Lord held with the rich young ruler (Matt. 19:16–22). This wealthy young man who had already attained sufficient pre-eminence to be elected a member of the synagogue, could not find satisfaction in either his position or his possessions, so he confronted the Master with his problem. The Teacher tested him out by telling him to keep the Commandments, to which the young man responded that he had done so from his youth. Then discerning the heart of the difficulty, which was covetousness, our Lord said to him, "If thou wilt be perfect, go and sell that thou hast, and give to the poor, and thou shalt have treasure in heaven; and come and follow me." However, his love for his possessions outweighed even his desire for life, and he went away sorrowful. The Teacher let the young man make his own choice, and in this case it was a refusal rather than an acceptance.

c. The disputation

When confronted by enemies and accusers, Christ adopted the method of disputation. These disputations were controversial in form and searching in character. The purpose of His enemies was to entangle Him in His talk by asking hard questions. But He never appears at a disadvantage, is never taken unawares.

When the Pharisees challenged the authority of Jesus, He turned upon them with a question they found themselves unable to answer: "The baptism of John, whence was it? from heaven, or from men?" (Matt. 21:25). This question put His enemies into a predicament. If they had answered, "From heaven," our Lord would have replied, "Well, why did you not believe in him?" If they had said, "From men," they would have endangered their lives, for the people had a high regard for John the Baptist, and believed that he was all he claimed to be. So the Pharisees declared they could not answer, and in making this response they confessed their ignorance and cowardice.

In that last week of His ministry, He was viciously assaulted by representatives of the three political groups (Herodians, Sadducees, and Pharisees) with many perplexing questions. When He had successfully silenced His critics, He took the offensive and propounded a baffling question: "What think ye of Christ? whose son is he? They say unto him, The son of David." Whereupon our Lord asked His unanswerable question: "How then doth David in spirit call him Lord, saying, The Lord said unto my Lord, Sit thou on my right hand, till I make thine enemies thy footstool? If David then call him Lord, how is he his son?" (Matt. 22:41–46). The Pharisees were unable to answer this question without acknowledging the deity of Jesus Christ. With what marvelous skill did He use the Old Testament to effectively silence His enemies!

d. The parable

It is the use of the parable in His teaching by which our Lord is most widely known. In fact they have been called the consummation of His art. About one-fourth of His words, as recorded by Mark, and about one-half as recorded by Luke, are in parable form. If the parables were omitted from His teaching, much of it would be gone, and if He had not used the method, He would not have been nearly so effective. He seems to have taken up the parable suddenly, about the middle of His ministry.[8] The parable of the sower was the first one

[8] Hinsdale, *op. cit.,* p. 161.

He uttered, and from that time on He used the parable so frequently we read that "without a parable spake he not unto them" (Mark 4:34).

One needs to read Matthew thirteen to fully understand the purpose of the parable. The disciples did not understand the hidden meaning the parable of the sower contained. In consequence, they came to Him afterward for the explanation, and it was in this connection that He gave the reason for His speaking to them in parables. "It is given unto you to know the mysteries of the kingdom of heaven, but to them it is not given . . . Therefore speak I to them in parables: because they seeing see not; and hearing they hear not, neither do they understand . . . For this people's heart is waxed gross, and their ears are dull of hearing, and their eyes they have closed; lest at any time they should see with their eyes and hear with their ears, and should understand with their heart, and should be converted, and I should heal them. But blessed are your eyes, for they see: and your ears, for they hear" (Matt. 13:11–18).

It is evident from this direct statement of our Lord that the parable was not used as a method of teaching because of its clearness and beauty. The parable was used to conceal truth, fully as much as to clarify it.[9] This required marvelous ability. To His enemies, who resisted and refused the truth, the parable would appear as an innocent story. To the cognizant disciples, however, it conveyed important truth.

The reason for this is apparent. Our Lord wished to instruct His disciples in public as well as in private. It was impossible therefore, for Him to escape the scribes and Pharisees, who were plotting to put Him to death. That they might not find evidence upon which to base an accusation against Him, He withheld from their understanding the great truths

[9] Hinsdale, *op. cit.,* p. 167.

His disciples alone could appreciate. It was only during the last week, when it was no longer necessary for Him to conceal His knowledge of their criminal intentions, that He uttered that outstanding denunciation against the scribes and Pharisees (Matthew 23). And He made His last parables so pointed that they grasped their true significance. After He had spoken the parable of the two sons, and the wicked husbandmen, we read, "When the chief priests and Pharisees had heard his parables, they perceived that He spake of them" (Matt. 21:45).

III. THE RESULTS OF HIS TEACHING

Our Lord must be recognized as a master teacher when judged by the results of His teaching. He left no book or written page behind Him. He bequeathed no system, no philosophy, no legislation. While He founded the Church, He trained others to establish it. During His ministry He devoted Himself primarily to the students He had enrolled in His training class. The results of His teaching were to be manifest in their lives and accomplishments.

And so it proved. It has been well said, "the greatest miracle in history seems to be the transformation that Jesus effected in the lives of His disciples." These disciples transformed by His teaching, His death, His resurrection, and the baptism of the Holy Spirit, went forth to turn the world up-side-down. Ten of them gave their lives as a testimony to their faith in their Teacher.

1. Lives Transformed

The men whom Jesus taught were far from perfect when they enrolled in His training class. Simon, who was to be given the name Peter, was not only ignorant, but impulsive and sinful. It was after Peter and John had performed a notable miracle in Jerusalem that we read, "When they saw the boldness of Peter and John, and perceived that they were unlearned and ignorant men, they marveled" (Acts 4:13). Peter was so reckless that he cut off the ear of the high priest's servant when the soldiers came to arrest his Lord. Peter probably aimed for the head but slashed off only an ear. It was the bungling attempt of an impetuous disciple. Peter's vulgar life came to the surface that night of His Lord's betrayal when he cursed and swore that he never knew Him.

John, too, was impetuous. He became so angry at the Samaritans who refused to provide Jesus entertainment that he asked his Teacher for permission to bring fire down from heaven and consume them. John and James, in their selfish ambitions to have the chief seats in our Lord's kingdom, brought down upon themselves the scorn and contempt of all the other disciples.

Simon the Zealot, as the title indicates, belonged to a radical political party and must have been regarded by outsiders as more of a liability than an asset to the cause.

Matthew was one of those much despised tax gatherers, and surely his presence could not have added any prestige to the group. Matthew, the publican, he calls himself—that was his occupation—and more, that was his character. He sets that mark of ignominy upon himself. He was recognized as a traitor to his country. In order to enrich himself, and to do so as quickly as possible, he joined hands with the oppressors of his people.

Judas was such a hard case that all the years of association with the Master proved to have no effect upon his character. He was already so far down the pathway of evil that although he was for three years in the best environment this world has ever provided, and even became the treasurer of the group, he yielded to his great greed for gain and sold his Master for thirty pieces of silver.

The transformation of character in the case of the disciples was accomplished so gradually and yet so completely that the courageous and consecrated men who occupied the stage in the Acts of the Apostles were altogether different from the untrained, uncouth, unlettered men who first enrolled in our Lord's training class. Peter is a man of faith—confident and aggressive. John becomes the beloved disciple who writes, "Little children, love one another." James is so zealous for the truth that he becomes first of the martyred disciples. Matthew, no longer scorned as publican and sinner, gives us the first of the Gospels.

2. Lives dedicated

As the result of our Lord's teaching, we find there soon existed between Him and His disciples a bond of union, a personal attachment so strong that they early left all that was dear to them in life that they might dedicate themselves to His service. There are several illustrations of this in the Gospel (cf. Mark 1:18, 20).

Since Peter was recognized as spokesman for the Twelve, it is not always plain whether he was expressing only his own personal feelings or those of the entire group. He seems to have spoken for all the disciples, on the occasion when the rich young ruler found that he was unable to meet the test of discipleship, and went away sorrowful. Peter had occasion to ask, "Behold, we have forsaken all, and followed thee; what shall we have therefore?" Jesus commends their loyalty, "Verily I say unto you, That ye which have followed me, in the regeneration when the Son of man shall sit in the throne of his glory, ye also shall sit upon twelve thrones, judging the twelve tribes of Israel" (Matt. 19:27, 28).

On another occasion in the synagogue of Capernaum our Lord's discourse gave such offense that many of His professed followers "went back, and walked no more with him." Jesus then put the test to the twelve, "Will ye also go away?" Peter replied in behalf of them all, "Lord, to whom shall we go? Thou hast the words of eternal life. And we believe and are sure that thou art that Christ, the Son of the living God" (John 6:66–69). The noble and explicit confession of loyalty and recognition of their Teacher as the Messiah was not long after repeated on another occasion, at Caesarea Philippi.

Thomas expressed his loyalty in the later days of our Lord's ministry. By this time it was well known that danger lurked in the city of Jerusalem. In fact, the last time our Lord had been in Jerusalem the angry Jews had taken up stones to hurl at Him. It was only by a miracle that He escaped out of their hands and retired with His disciples into a secluded place. But at last to this desert spot came tidings of the death of Lazarus in Bethany, near Jerusalem. Jesus resolved to return; the disciples were startled. They reminded Him, "Master, the Jews of late sought to stone thee; and goest thou thither again?" But when He insisted upon making this journey which was to prove His last, Thomas said unto his fellow disciples, "Let us also go, that we may die with him" (John 11:8–16).

That was a most noble sentiment, for the disciple meant every word of it. It was a cruel death and his flesh shrank from it. He saw death in all its hardness, cruelty and pain, and yet his devotion to his Lord was so great that he said, "Let us also go, that we may die with him." He expressed a fervor of love that is faithful unto death, a loyal devotion that only in the presence of peril asserts its full strength and nobility.

When James and John and their ambitious mother felt that the hour of the coming kingdom was at hand, they asked a great favor. "Command," says the mother, "that these, my two sons, may sit, one on thy right hand, and one on thy left hand in thy kingdom" (Matt. 20:20–28, R.V.). Thus they exposed their vain ambitions, and at the same time their blindness to spiritual values, and their ignorance of the true nature of the honors and rewards in Christ's kingdom. In that kingdom every true and faithful follower of Jesus must, in some sense, drink of His cup and be baptized with His baptism. And so, Jesus asked the sons of Zebedee if they were able to fulfill these conditions of service; had they the moral and the spiritual power to walk in His footsteps. It was a searching question and it brought out again the nobler side of their characters. Even if their confident answer betrayed an improper knowledge of what the cup and the baptism meant, it at any rate proved to Christ their implicit trust and their splendid devotion to His cause. To walk in His steps and share in His experiences—that was the only life they cared to live. Not, therefore, with foolish boasting, but with the daring of a great love, they answered, "We are able." In a few years, when the testing time came, both of these disciples proved that they were able, and did not shrink from the ordeal of persecution and death itself.

3. Lives multiplied

The results of our Lord's teaching were further manifested by the multiplication of the men whom He chose to be His disciples. He wrought His ideals into their characters so they in turn were able to pass on these same ideals to others. His school of the Twelve became the Christian Church. The Acts of the Apostles reads like the Gospels. It is a record of living over the Master Teacher's life and ministry. The apostles "entered into the temple about daybreak and taught." "Everyday in the temple and at home they ceased not to teach and to preach." The apostles preached, taught, bore witness, testified, argued, and exhorted. In this ministry they multiplied themselves.

Andrew began his ministry in his own home. "He first findeth his own brother Simon, and saith unto him, We have found the Messias, which is, being interpreted, the Christ. And he brought him to Jesus" (John 1:41, 42). But Andrew's labors were not confined to his own home. He was the means of introducing to Jesus those Greeks that were anxious to see Him. They were the first-fruits of our Lord among the Gentiles. In vision He saw the kingdom stretched from shore to shore, and from the river unto the ends of the earth, and it was Andrew who brought them. It seems that Philip was undecided until he had consulted Andrew. But the latter seems to have better understood his Teacher. He felt that Jesus would be glad to help and save anyone (John 12:20–22).

When Philip became a disciple and enrolled in our Lord's training class, he felt constrained to look up Nathanael. Nathanael was not so easily won by Philip, as was Simon by Andrew. Pious in heart as he was, and ready to accept the fulfillment of Scripture, he had certain preconceived ideas which prevented his immediate assent to Philip's good tidings. But Philip did not argue with his friend. He took a shorter course. He was convinced that if Nathanael could only see Jesus, speak with Him, breathe the atmosphere that surrounded Him, all prejudices would be removed. So he simply said, "Come and see" (John 1:45, 46).

Peter was a recognized leader in the early Church, and his remarkable sermon on the Day of Pentecost resulted in the first three thousand members being added to the faithful one hundred and twenty who had prayed ten days for that remarkable day of the Church's origin. The first part of the Acts of the Apostles is in reality the acts of Peter, since he was the acknowledged leader in the early days of the Church. Later when he left Rome, John Mark accompanied him, and it was largely from his listening to the repeated accounts of Peter's teaching and preaching that he came to write the Gospel of Mark. Later Peter wrote the First and Second Epistles, which have his name, warning the Church, first of the enemies without, and second of the enemies within.

When Matthew rose up and left all to enter our Lord's training class, the only things he took with him out of his old occupation were his pen and ink (Matt. 9:9). The Gospel of Matthew, which has been printed in more than one thousand different languages and dialects, represents Matthew's contribution of his pen and ink. After the record of the feast he prepared for our Lord and His disciples (Luke 5:27–32), he disappears from history. No more is heard of him in the New Testament. But by virtue of the Gospel which he was inspired to write, he is today one of the chief benefactors of the human race.

4. Lives Sacrificed

All but one of the eleven disciples who attended our Lord's school gave their lives in witness of their faith in Him, as well as their firm belief in His instruction. The martyrdom of only one is recorded in Scripture, while a second writes of his anticipated execution; but from other sources, considered reliable, there is a record of the death of the others.

a. James the son of Zebedee (Acts 12:2)

Despite the fact that John appears the more active of the two sons of Zebedee in the early Church, it was James that Herod executed in prison with a sword, although he was thwarted by the prevailing prayers of the Church from putting Peter to death in the same way (Acts 12:3–11). Thus the first of the apostles partook of the cup he had long since told his Lord he was ready to drink (Matt. 20:22).

b. James the son of Alphaeus

Josephus, the Jewish historian, states that this disciple, after a ministry of some years in Jerusalem, was thrown from a lofty pinnacle of the temple, but not being killed by the fall recovered himself sufficiently to pray fervently for his murderers.

Accordingly, his enemies, vexed that they had not fully accomplished their work, poured a shower of stones upon him, and one more merciful than the rest put an end to his suffering with a fuller's club.

c. Bartholomew

Bartholomew was the first missionary to India, according to tradition, and after spending considerable time in the eastern extremities of Asia, he returned to labor in Phrygia and Lycaonia where, Chrysostom assures us, he instructed and trained up the inhabitants in the Christian discipline. His last days were spent at Albanople in Armenia where the magistrates, provoked by his preaching, prevailed upon the governor to put him to death.

d. Jude

Paulinus tells us that Jude, or Thaddeus, traveled up and down Judea and Galilee; then through Samaria into Idumaea and to the cities of Arabia, and afterwards to Syria and Mesopotamia. The writers of the Latin church are unanimous in declaring that he extended his ministry into Persia, where he was so outspoken in reproving the superstitious rites and customs that he was cruelly put to death.

e. Thomas

Thomas first went into Ethiopia, but later followed Bartholomew into India. At Mattapour, not far from the mouth of the Ganges, he began to erect a place for divine worship until prohibited by the idolatrous priests. At a small distance from the city was a tomb whither the apostle was accustomed to retire for devotions. Hither the priests followed him, and while he was in prayer, shot at him with arrows, then ran a lance through his body.

f. Andrew

Andrew traveled over Thrace, Macedonia, Thessaly, Achaia, and Epirus preaching the gospel and confirming the doctrine with signs and miracles. At last he came to Petrea, a city of Achaia, where he gave his last and greatest testimony, sealing it with his blood. The apostle was first scourged by seven lictors and then crucified. He was fastened to two pieces of timber crossing each other in the center in the form of the letter X, and hence usually known by the name of St. Andrew's cross.

g. Simon the zealot

Less is known of Simon's ministry than that of any other apostle, but he is said to have penetrated the remote, barbarous countries of Africa, sustaining great hardships and persecutions, and to have been crucified.

h. Matthew

Matthew labored first among the Jews in different parts of Judaea, and later heard the call to the regions beyond. Before he left he was entreated by the Jewish converts to write up the ministry, death, and resurrection of the Lord Jesus Christ and leave the record with them as an enduring monument of what he had so often delivered to them in his teaching. This accounts for the preparation of the Gospel according to Matthew, the only Gospel to be written in Hebrew.

After leaving Judaea, he traveled into Africa and ministered to the Ethiopians, and after laboring indefatigably, he suffered martyrdom, being slain with a halberd.

i. Peter

Peter, who was so active in establishing the Jerusalem church, appears later to have made Joppa his headquarters, where he raised Dorcas from the dead and received the call to Caesarea for his conference with the Roman centurian, Cornelius (Acts, chapters 9, 10). Later he returned to Jerusalem, where he was arrested and imprisoned by Herod who planned to execute him at the conclusion of the Passover. But God had other plans for him, and he was miraculously delivered by an angel on the eve of his martyrdom (Acts 12:1-19). After this, Caesarea was his residence until the meeting of the first Church council at Jerusalem, which he attended and in which he took an active part (Acts 15:7-11). Here the Bible writer leaves him, but we hear of him later at Babylon where he wrote his First Epistle. Ambrose tells us that he was in Rome at the time of Nero's persecution of the Christians, and for nine months was confined in prison, from which he wrote his Second Epistle. In this last writing he seems to have had a premonition of his execution (II Peter 1:14, 15). Instead of being beheaded, like Paul, he was sentenced to be crucified. Upon arrival at the place of execution, he requested that he might be nailed to the cross head downwards, affirming that he was unworthy to suffer in the same position in which his Lord had been crucified. Thus the leader of the apostolic group probably suffered the most agonizing death of all.

j. John

John was the only one of the disciples that did not experience a violent death. He was the youngest of the group and lived long after all the others had passed off the scene. It will be remembered that this disciple whom Jesus loved was assigned the care of His mother (John 19:26, 27), and it probably was not until her death that John felt free to leave Jerusalem. Asia appears to have been his field, for here he founded many churches. His chief place of residence was at Ephesus, where Paul had already founded a church. When Domitian began his persecution of the Christians, John was ordered to Rome where, according to Tertullian, he was thrown into a caldron of boiling oil, from which he miraculously escaped, only to be transported to the lonely island of Patmos; there, about the end of Domitian's reign, he wrote the Book of the Revelation.

Upon the death of Domitian, there was a spirit of tolerance

shown the Christians, and the apostle was released from Patmos and permitted to return to Ephesus, exercising the office of bishop which was first held by the martyred Timothy. Now over ninety years of age, he spent his last days in an indefatigable execution of his charge, traveling from east to west in Asia Minor and composing the Gospel and three Epistles that have come down to us. Death finally put an end to his labors in the ninety-eighth year of his life, and according to Eusebius he was buried near Ephesus. Like Daniel, the beloved prophet of the Old Testament, John not only outlived the emperors, as well as the disciples, but was accorded the most far-reaching visions of the future.

The test of the teacher and his teaching, we are again reminded, is what happens in the lives of his disciples. Our Lord fully met this all-exacting test in the unparalleled response of His disciples. Their lives were transformed, dedicated, multiplied and eventually sacrificed for their Teacher and the great task to which He had commissioned them.

QUESTIONS

1. In what five respects was our Lord prepared to be a teacher?
2. State five facts as evidence that our Lord was recognized as a teacher.
3. Name three characteristics of a teacher.
4. Give four illustrations of His mastery of the Scripture.
5. In His relation to others, on what three occasions did our Lord show His knowledge of human nature?
6. Name four methods that were employed by the Master Teacher.
7. What illustrations can be given to show that His instruction looked to a practical end?
8. Define and illustrate the discourse method.
9. Compare the dialogue with disputation methods and give illustration of each.

10. What was the purpose of the parable?
11. In what respects were the lives of His disciples transformed?
12. Name four results of His teaching.
13. Give an illustration of the devotion of the disciples.
14. In what respect were the lives of the disciples multiplied?
15. How did the disciples sacrifice their lives?

Bibliography

All Bible Graded Series, Scripture Press, Chicago.

Benson, Clarence H.—*The Sunday School in Action,* Moody Press, Chicago, 1928.

Berkeley, James Percival—*You Can Teach,* Judson Press, Philadelphia, 1941.

Betts, George Herbert—*How to Teach Religion,* The Abingdon Press, Nashville, Tenn., 1910.

Brumbaugh, Martin G.—*The Making of a Teacher,* Harper & Bros., New York, 1932.

Burrell, D. J., *The Wonderful Teacher,* Fleming H. Revell Co., New York, 1902.

Carmack, H. E.—*How to Teach the Sunday School Lesson,* Fleming H. Revell, 1911.

Coleman, Frank G.—*The Romance of Winning Children,* Union Gospel Press, Cleveland, 1948.

Dobbins, Gaines S.—*The Improvement of Teaching in the Sunday School,* Sunday School Board, Southern Baptist Convention, Nashville, Tenn., 1943.

Eavey, C. B.—*Principles of Teaching for Christian Teachers,* Zondervan Publishing House, Grand Rapids, Mich., 1940.

Gregory, John Milton—*The Seven Laws of Teaching,* Pilgrim Press, Boston, 1917.

Hinsdale, B. A.—*Jesus As a Teacher,* Christian Board of Education, Philadelphia, 1917.

Kuist, Howard Tillman—*The Pedagogy of St. Paul,* Geo. H. Doran Company, New York, 1925.

Mathewson, Lester B.—*The Illustration in Sermon, Address, Conversation and Teaching,* Fleming H. Revell Co., 1936.

McKinney, A. H.—*Practical Pedagogy in the Sunday School,* Fleming H. Revell Co., 1911.

—*A Top-Notch Teacher,* W. A. Wilde Co., Boston, 1925.

McKoy, Charles Francis—*The Art of Jesus As a Teacher*, The Judson Press, 1930.

Norlie, O. M.—*An Elementary Christian Psychology*, Augsburg Publishing House, Minneapolis, 1924.

Piper, David R.—*How Would Jesus Teach?* David C. Cook Publishing Co., Elgin, Ill., 1931.

Plummer, L. Flora—*The Soul-Winning Teacher*, Fleming H. Revell Co., 1934.

Price, J. M.—*Jesus the Teacher*, The Sunday School Board of the Southern Baptist Convention, Nashville, Tenn., 1946.

Reu, Dr. M.—*How to Teach in the Sunday School*, The Lutheran Book Concern, Columbus, Ohio, 1939.

Schmauk, Theodore E.—*How to Teach in Sunday School*, The United Lutheran Publication House, Philadelphia, 1920.

Spurgeon, Charles Haddon—*Sermons*, Vol. II, "Teaching Children."

Trumbull, H. Clay—*Teaching and Teachers*, Charles Scribner's Sons, New York, 1915.

White, Goodrich C.—*Teaching in the Sunday School*, Cokesbury Press, Nashville, Tenn., 1929.

Note: A number of the books in this list are obtainable second hand only.